The Women of Death Row

Georgia Spinola

Published by Trellis Publishing, 2021.

While every precaution has been taken in the preparation of this book, the publisher assumes no responsibility for errors or omissions, or for damages resulting from the use of the information contained herein.

THE WOMEN OF DEATH ROW

First edition. July 8, 2021.

Copyright © 2021 Georgia Spinola.

ISBN: 979-8224481682

Written by Georgia Spinola.

THE WOMEN OF DEATH ROW

1

Georgia Spinola

VELMA BULLARD

It never ends.

No way.

No way am I letting this man demean and degrade me another day.

He's just like my father.

A binge drinker. And the binges were happening more and more.

He's on the road to nowhere and taking me with him.

It never ends.

First my father. Now him.

Fuck it.

I threw the cigarette on the blanket. I knew it was flammable.

Then I watched the smoke rise and smiled.

In Lumberton, North Carolina, Thomas Burke fell victim to a house fire which was caused by a burning cigarette. Investigative authorities thought that he had fallen asleep while smoking, leaving thirty-eight-year-old Velma Burke as his widow.

They didn't know that the fire was set by Velma.

Velma knew how to play the part of the grieving widow. She cried and gave the authorities the requisite crocodile tears. No one would believe that the murder of Thomas Burke would set off a series of killings performed by the seemingly kind and harmless church-going woman with the soft voice.

EARLY LIFE

Velma Bullard grew up as the second of nine children in the rural part of Sampson County, North Carolina.

Times were tough for the Bullard family. They would live on a small farm with no electricity, running water or an outhouse.

"They had to go outdoors," forensic psychologist Paula Orange said. "The entire family had to endure the indignity of going into the woods or using pots to shit and piss."

The home was small and cramped for the nine children. Velma would be forced to sleep in the same bedroom with her parents until the age of five.

Her father was a loom repairman (fixing an apparatus that was used to weave clothing) and an abusive alcoholic. Velma had an older brother, Olive, who were subject to his nightly beatings. Lillie, her mother, was too meek to protect her children from her husband's violent outbursts.

"She had the type of father who would not need any provocation," Orange said. "He would take out the pettiest frustrations, like not being able to find something around the house, and take it out on the children. Velma would become resentful toward her mother who was too weak or indifferent to stop her father from beating on the kids. She accepted his discipline as 'the way it was.'"

Velma would find school as a welcome escape from her dreadful home life. She loved her teacher and was an excellent student during her early grade school years. When she would return home from school, she took solace in the fact that her father would always arrive home late as he worked long hours at the textile mill.

"Her father Murphy had that Protestant work ethic in him," Orange said. "He accepted the long hours and low pay, seeing a kind of nobility in that. Only problem was, he would binge drink. Not store bought alcohol but homemade moonshine. After a couple of shots, he would be 'lit' and inflict his wrath on everyone in the house."

By the age of eleven, Velma would be forced to take on various chores around the farm. She would clean up the house, washing and iron everyone's clothing (eleven people). Her father would chastise her for not mending or sewing his work clothes properly as well.

"Her father was a stern taskmaster," Orange said. "Hell, you can say 'slave driver.' He would have Velma come home early from school days when the laundry got too backed up. Velma hated this and felt embarrassed. Her family didn't have much and as she grew older her classmates began to see her for what she was, a poor girl that was an easy mark for teasing."

Velma would grow to be 5'3" but gain weight as she got older. She would be mocked about her obesity, her shoddy clothes the gap between her two front teeth. She would also be called "knot head" after she ran head first into a boy at school which left a permanent contusion on her forehead.

By the age of twelve, Velma seemed to have taken on all of her mother's duties. She would cook all of the family meals in addition to performing cleaning around the farm house. She would miss school for days at a time as her father forced her to complete chores around the home before she could continue her education.

"Academic achievement was not at the forefront of her father's mind," Orange said. "Her mother was of little use because of her depression and mental illness. Velma was the oldest girl so she took on the duties of mom at an age where she should have been playing with dolls."

ANGER, ABUSE, AND CHURCH

Despite her father's verbal abuse and alcohol-fueled beatings, the family kept up a face of religious interest. Velma would be sent to Bible school every year until the age of thirteen. During her last year of Bible school, her father marked the occasion by buying Velma a silk pink dress with ribbons. Velma recalled the day as one of the happiest of her life.

The happiness would be short-lived.

Velma would claim that her father raped her when she was thirteen years old. She revealed this only to her pastor in her later years before she stood trial. Velma did not even tell her mother whom she did not think would believe the molestation took place.

"Things that went on inside our home when I grew up," Velma said. "Were kept inside."

At the age of fifteen, Velma continued to excel in school. Despite her chubby physique, she becomes adept at basketball and is pegged to be the team's star player for the upcoming season. But her father did not allow her to play.

"Who is going to iron these damn clothes?" he snarled.

The family then moved to Robeson county and switched from the Presbyterian denomination to Baptist. It was here that Velma would meet Thomas Burke and the two made it clear that they wanted to date. Once again, Velma's father would intervene, telling Velma that she had to wait until her sixteenth birthday until she could date.

The two waited patiently for her birthday to arrive and the following year Thomas would propose to her while they went to the movies.

Knowing that her father would not approve, Velma and Thomas eloped, moving to Dillon, South Carolina. Neither Thomas or Velma had any money as they both quit high school to get married. Thomas then went to work at a local textile mill.

"At this point, I believe that Velma began to realize that her life would not be that much better with Thomas," Orange said. "He literally has the same job as her father."

Economics forced Velma and Thomas to move in with his parents. This arrangement would last for a year until Thomas got a better paying job at a soft drink company.

At the age of nineteen, Velma would give birth to her first son, Ronnie. The couple would then move back to Parkton, North Carolina where they would remain in the same home for eleven years. Two years later, the young couple would welcome a daughter named Kim.

A CYCLE OF RELIGION AND ABUSE

The Burkes would be fixtures at the local Baptist church with Velma taking the reigns to teach a Sunday school class. But the prayers and sermons would do little to offset the growing ennui in the Burke home. Two years after giving birth to Kim, Velma would get hit by a drunk driver while crossing the street. She would be hospitalized for an extended period, suffering both physically and mentally.

Thomas' job at the soft drink company would not be enough to provide for the family. Velma would be forced to leave her small children at home and work in a textile mill just like her father. The couple would have different work hours, with Velma working nights and Thomas working days as they would take turns watching the children.

Velma would fall victim to the hard work at the mill and the stress of raising two young children. She began bleeding and her doctor performed a hysterectomy.

Velma's mother would take pity on the couple and give them one acre of land near their old farm. Thomas would build a three-bedroom home for the family but Velma was already going down a slippery slope. Her personality changed after the hysterectomy, claiming that she always felt "nervous and afraid."

Things would get worse as Thomas suffered a head injury in a car accident. He then began to drink heavily and begin to beat Velma.

"It was deja vu," Orange said. "Velma had, in essence, married her father."

One night, the couple argued and Thomas punched Velma in an alcohol-fueled tantrum. The police are called to the home and Velma sent Thomas to the state hospital to get treatment for his drinking. Her husband remains there for three days but when he returns home, his behavior is worse than behavior. He's angry at Velma for sending him to the "drunk tank". His alcoholism worsens and he would go on to lose his job because of absenteeism.

"Velma is thirty-five years old at this time," Orange said. "But she's an old thirty-five with crow's feet under her eyes and a hangdog look. She's had a rough life, not necessarily by her own design, and it has taken its toll."

Velma leaves the textile mill but then finds two different jobs in order to support the family. During the day, she works as a sales clerk in a Belk department store. At night, she goes to work as a machine operator in a cotton mill.

Thomas, meanwhile, would continue to drink.

He rages on a daily basis, on one occasion he pinned son Ronnie up against the wall and threatened him with a knife. Velma would faint during the encounter and be transported to the hospital. She was diagnosed as having a nervous breakdown and lapsed into a serious depression. The medical staff gave her tranquilizers to calm down. Velma believed that it was during this stint in the hospital that she became addicted to the painkillers.

"The drugs were helping," Orange said. "When nothing else did. So she wanted more and more."

Velma's children acknowledged that their mother's mood swings were due to the drugs.

Over the next three years, Velma would go in and out of the hospital for drug overdoses. After each visit, her addiction only grew as did her prescription list.

"She fell through the cracks in her own family," Orange said. "And in the system itself. Her family had their own issues to deal with as Thomas would abuse everyone on a daily basis. Finally, Velma did something she could control. She killed her husband."

On April 21st, 1969, Velma would drop a cigarette on the floor of her home and waited until her husband inhaled enough smoke to die.

His death, however, would do nothing to solve Velma's problems.

Her addictions and anxiety would only get worse.

A HOSPITAL FREQUENT FLYER

Velma would have another nervous breakdown after killing Thomas and lapse into a guilt-ridden depression. But seven months later, a co-worker at the Belk department store would introduce her to fifty-four-year-old Jennings Barfield. Jennings had emphysema and diabetes but Velma would marry him anyway. Unlike her marriage with Thomas which started out well, Velma's marriage with the older Jennings would be troubled from the start. Her drug addiction would escalate and Jennings would express his own regret at marrying her.

"I don't know why I married her," Jennings said. "All she does is pop pills all day."

After less than three years of marriage, Velma decided to part ways with Jennings. She didn't file for divorce, however, she decided to poison him with arsenic. She would later claim that she only meant to "make him sick."

Jennings Barfield was already ill and doctors had no suspicion that Velma was behind the death. Arsenic was a slow burn poison that could kill without detection. The autopsy called for no arsenic test and Velma had gotten away with murder once again.

But Seven months later, Velma would overdose on her prescription meds and become hospitalized. Her family recognized the pattern but could not wean Velma off of the drinks. She would remain hospitalized for three weeks.

Her personality seemed to change after the hospital release. She returned to work at Belk department store but kept being combative and argumentative with customers. Her boss knew of her circumstances and tried to coax her to do better. He took her away from the public contact and into the back stock room where he had her put pricing on the clothing items.

Her boss soon realized that Velma's addiction had gotten out of control. Velma would not be able to function in the back room, leaving tasks uncompleted as she would have her prescription medications delivered to the store.

"It is a hopeless situation," the store manager told Velma's son Ronnie before he fired his mother.

BROKE AND DESTITUTE

With no income, Velma would lose the family home as she no longer paid the mortgage. She would be forced to move back in with her parents and face the two people she blamed everything for.

Her father had grown ill, however, and would die from lung cancer shortly after Velma moved back into the home. She would feel bad about her father's death and admit that she had a love/hate relationship with him.

"I had learned to love him as much as I had hated him," Velma said. "He was so good to my kids. I think he tried to do with my kids like he wished he had done to us. He could not stand to see me correct them. If I would pick them up and spank them, he would ask me, 'Isn't that enough?'"

But after her father's death Velma self-medicated once again. She overdosed and was hospitalized for two weeks. Her family didn't judge, they instead thought she was "cursed."

"Velma needed psychiatric help," Orange said. "So she began medicating herself with deleterious results. She would "doctor shop" for different physicians who would be manipulated into giving her the drugs she wanted. Her addiction eventually grows until she becomes desperate for money in order to fuel the drug habit."

A MURDERER AND A THIEF

Velma began stealing from those closest to her, starting with her mother. Her mother confronted Velma about a missing check and Velma went ballistic.

"She had violent mood swings," Orange said. "The medication had completely changed her personality as she needed the drugs above all else. The people around her were not familiar with how to handle a person who had this kind of mental illness. So this made for a very dangerous cocktail for her and anyone close to her."

Hitting a new low, Velma took out a $1,000 loan under her mother Lillie's name. She put up the family home as collateral and forged her mother's signature on the documents. Velma then blew through the money and a month later took out another loan, once again using her mother's house as collateral. The following month, she emptied the checking account on her now deceased husband, Jennings. Two months later, the loan company began sending Velma overdue notices as she had not been paying off the loan.

"In Velma's mind," Orange said. "She had no other choice but to kill off her own mother."

Velma went to the local pharmacy and looked for bottles that had the warning of "fatal if ingested." She put the poison into a drink for her mother and watched as she drank the fatal elixir.

Her mother then began vomiting and lost control of her bowels. Within a few hours, her mother could not so much as walk and an ambulance was called.

Velma came to visit her in the hospital to finish the job. Armed with a Thermos, she made a special concoction of chicken soup and arsenic.

"Drink it slow," Velma said as she tenderly lifted the cups to the lips of her ailing mother. "Slow."

Her mother would eventually die of "natural causes" as no one suspected Velma of committing murder. Instead, she received sympathy.

"So sorry for your loss," hospital staff said.

"The thing with arsenic is that it shuts down the whole system," Orange said. "So hospital staff just chalked up her mother's weakness to old age. Checking for arsenic poisoning would be the furthest thing from their mind."

Velma showed the necessary emotion and received sympathy from friends and family. She then moved in with her daughter Kim and son-in-law Dennis who lived in a trailer park. She could not evade the authorities for long though as the authorities caught wind of Velma's check forgeries.

Velma reacted as she always did. She would run away and medicate herself.

"Her drug addiction kept pushing her into a corner and she saw no way out," Orange said. "So, this time, she goes to her son Ronnie's house and overdoses again, trying to kill herself. She falls and breaks her collar bone which laid her out in the hospital another three weeks."

But the police find her situation unsympathetic.

"We're sorry, Velma," the deputy informed her at her hospital bed. "But once you have been cleared for release, we will arrest you."

Velma would not have that. She tried to overdose again but this go around the hospital staff pumped out her stomach.

She was sent to court the next day and sentenced to six months in jail for the forgery. She is released after four months for good behavior.

NO REHAB HERE

Her addiction still unchecked, Velma returned to live with Kim and her son-in-law. She rummaged through the belongings of her son-in-law and stole a check, forging his name so she can get more prescription meds. Her daughter Kim now has caught wind of her mother's addiction, pleading with her doctors to stop prescribing her.

"In some ways," Orange said. "The doctors were just as guilty as she was. But back in the day, there was no way to cross-reference this stuff like we do now. Once she had her fill with one doctor she would go to the next and the next."

Velma's addiction prevented her from taking a forty-hour a week job. So she looked for alternative forms of income.

She would find a job taking care of the elderly.

Montgomery and Dolly Edwards would be her first clients.

"She found herself some easy targets," Orange said. "There didn't seem to be any legislative body in place that prevents sociopaths from caretaking the elderly. So Velma doesn't slip through any cracks, she just befriends the elderly couple and begins taking care of them."

Montgomery was blind and unable to walk. He was 93-years old and his 83-year old wife was too feeble to take care of him. They paid $75 a week for Velma to become their live-in caretaker.

All was good, at least in the beginning. But Dolly had a sharp tongue and would criticize Velma daily. Velma would keep a nice exterior unless confronted, saw Dolly has yet another wheel in her cycle of verbal abuse.

"It seemed to be a never-ending loop for her," Orange said. "Being forced to deal with verbally abusive people. Velma had long since snapped and Dollie simply had no idea who she was dealing with."

Velma began to plot out Montgomery and Dollie's demise until she meets their nephew, Stuart Taylor.

Stuart was already married but was blown away when he met the caretaker of his Aunt Dollie.

Velma would play it cool, stealing what she could from the couple in terms of petty cash and household items that had value. They outlived their usefulness to her within a year as Montgomery died of "natural causes". One month later, Dolly also passed away.

And again, no one suspected the sweet and soft-spoken Velma to have had anything to do with their deaths.

MOVING ON

Velma saw being a caretaker as a perfect front for her. She could steal as much money as she could and when the old folks detected something amiss she would simply poison them. After killing the Edwards' couple, she set the word out at church that she as available to be a caregiver. The pastor would refer her to Margie Lee Pittman who was seeking for a caregiver for her elderly parents, John Henry and Record Lee.

"She comes here twice a week," the pastor reassured Pittman. "She's a nice, kindly woman. You can't go wrong."

Pittman's father, John Henry Lee, was eighty years old when he discovered that his new caregiver had forged a $50 check on his account. He then fell violently ill, suffering through a spastic spell of vomiting, diarrhea, and convulsions. The doctors would chalk up his quick death to gastroenteritis but in fact, he had been poisoned with arsenic.

Velma played the caregiver role until his end. She attended his funeral and cried with the family, sending an ornate wreath (with money stolen from the dead man) to the proceedings.

For whatever reason, Velma spared Lee's wife and moved back to Lumberton, North Carolina to live in a trailer park. She began working as an aide in a nursing home and received word from Stuart that he was now a widow. The two began dating and she moved part of her belongings into his home.

"Stuart is a nice guy," Orange said. "He has no idea what kind of woman Velma is. She is so manipulative and cunning that the younger man is putty in her hands. So the relationship starts great as she reels him in with kindness and charm."

The couple are happy cohabitating until Stuart Stuart finds a letter addressed to Velma from the state penitentiary.

Curious, he began reading the correspondence and realized that is from a former cellmate of Velma.

Stuart became enraged. He threatened to "expose" Velma to all of his family and friends. Somehow, someway, however, she was able to calm him down.

He then found out that she had forged over $200 in checks on his account. The two argued but stayed together for the next two months.

"Velma had the Christian facade down pat," Orange said. "She asked Stuart to forgive her and the next thing you know they are going to a Rex Humbard revival. But before they went, she poured arsenic poison in both his beer and tea. She made sure he drank every drop."

Returning home from the revival, Stuart started to vomit on the drive home, the poison kicking in.

Velma had to keep the con going. She had to appear like a concerned girlfriend so she called up Stuart's daughter, Alice, later that night and told her that Stuart had came down with the flu.

Stuart's daughter expressed concern but Velma kept her at bay.

"Don't you worry now, honey. I'll take care of everything."

Stuart died the next day.

Velma would speak at Stuart's funeral and tearfully asked for his wedding band. His family graciously allowed her to have it and gave her $400 to help her cope with the grief.

But Alice knew her father was a picture of health. She vociferously argued for more tests beyond the standard autopsy and sure enough, arsenic had been found in Stuart's tissues.

On March 10th, 1978, the sheriffs arrived at Velma's home to bring her in for questioning. She was interrogated for over three hours, holding her ground. But she knows the evidence will trump her denials and tries to commit suicide after being released. This go around, however, her son Ronnie stopped her.

The sheriffs come to visit Velma again and she has one more surprise up her sleeve.

But Velma has one more surprise up her sleeve.

She would confess. Not only for the murder of Stuart but of six others.

"I set my first husband on fire," Velma confessed without an attorney present. "And I killed the rest of them."

"It was almost as if she wanted to be free of the guilt she had been carrying," Orange said. "Her confession seemed to take a burden off her back."

"The last ten years were like that," Velma said. "A drug nightmare. It was a case of not knowing where you are or what you've done."

The bodies of her victims were later exhumed and all tested positive for arsenic.

FACING THE GRIM REAPER

Velma's case would be prosecuted by Joe Freeman Britt, who was listed in the Guinness Book of World Records as the country's "deadliest prosecutor."

Velma would plead not guilty by reason of insanity but the court denied her plea.

"I needed to keep them sick until I could pay back the money I had stolen from them," Velma said. "I wanted to earn their thanks by nursing them back to health. I needed the money. I was addicted to pain killers. Anti-depressants. Amphetamines."

On November 23rd, 1978, Velma's trial would begin in Elizabethtown, North Carolina where she would be charged with the first-degree murder of her boyfriend, Stuart Taylor. The trial lasted seven days and the jury reached a verdict of guilty, placing her on death row at the age of 47. She was scheduled to be executed on February 3rd, 1979 but received a stay.

Velma would be sentenced to death and the verdict was appealed all the way to the U.S. Supreme court. Her attorney maintained that the jury had never been presented with the full extent of Velma's "addiction and background." Velma remained tight-lipped about that to everyone but her pastor. Her attorney felt thought her horrific background could have been used as part of her defense and the jury would have found her to be more of a sympathetic case.

CHANGING SPOTS?

"She's not the same person who went to prison in 1978," Kim Burke Norton, Velma's daughter said.

While in jail, Velma became a model prisoner.

"The first week I was here was the worst week," Velma recalled. "Everything about it."

Velma no longer had access to her drugs in prison and she began to dry out. With daily visits from two different pastors, Velma began to discuss her anger and repressed issues that fueled her addiction and murders.

Velma would claim that as she was awaiting trial in 1978 she came to a "meeting with Christ" that caused her to "change inwardly."

Velma heard a broadcast by radio evangelist JK Kinkle. "Jesus loves you, prisoners, too," Kinkle said. "He died for you too. No matter what you've done, the Lord will forgive you."

After Velma heard this sermon, she dropped to her knees and cried out to God.

She would then become the "go to" counselor for young inmates in the prison.

The inmates would nickname Velma as "Mama Margie" because of her wisdom and she would in turn think of them as her "adopted children."

The prison guards and counselors would take the most incorrigible prisoners and place them in a cell next to Velma. Velma would invariably counsel the young prisoner and advise them on the correct path.

"They'd come in ready to kill themselves," Sister Mary Teresa Floyd said. "And here she was with a death sentence, mothering and helping them."

"Living in prison is a struggle," Velma said. "Even at its best. And I know that without Him and His strength that has sustained me, I couldn't have made it even this far."

Her stay on death row soon became a part of the news brief. During this time, a phalanx of evangelists would take her cause to the mainstream. The Reverend Hugh Hoyle would become Velma's personal minister as she received stays of execution in September, October and December of 1981. She would also have a letter correspondence with Ruth Graham, Billy Graham's wife as well as meeting their daughter Ann.

While Velma impressed the Christian do-gooders, the family members of the victims were not taken in by her "conversion."

"She's got religion now, they say," Margie Lee Pittman said. "Well, she had religion before. So we all thought."

A few more stays were granted until 1984 when the U.S. Supreme Court justice Warren Burger granted her a stay until August of that year. At this point, however, her execution seemed inevitable. In an ironic move, Velma would choose poison rather than the gas chamber and enjoyed the final visits from her children and grandchildren.

During the final week before her execution, the Reverend Hoyle, and his wife came to the prison with a battery-powered portable keyboard. His wife played the little organ then the Reverend sang "He Hideth My Soul" and "He is So precious to Me" in the cramped visitor booth.

Velma sang along, whistling in the graveyard before the reaper came for her.

She then wrote letters to each of the victim's family asking them for forgiveness. Reverend Hoyle would deliver the letters to the families, all of whom would refuse them.

MEET THE HANGMAN

As her execution date neared, Velma was placed in a solitary cell that stood directly across from the death chamber.

"It's total isolation," Velma said. "From everyone I had been with for six years."

North Carolina Governor James B. Hunt would reject her final plea for clemency.

On the day of her execution, the jail house would turn into a media frenzy. Death penalty advocates gathered outside the prison and chanted "Hip, hip, hurrah...K-I-L-L" while some sloganeered with "burn, bitch, burn". The protesters held up a few placards that quote

Romans ch.13 which ironically was a verse that Velma would repeat to guards during her prison stay.

"For rulers are not a terror to good works, but to the evil...(The ruler) beareth no the sword in vain, for he is the minister of God, a revenger to execute wrath upon him that doeth evil."

The execution was scheduled to take place at 2:00 a.m but the protesters remained outside, their chants reduced to a simple "Kill her! Kill her!"

On November 2nd, 1984, Velma would be executed by lethal injection. The prison official came out and addressed the press, giving out copies of Barfield's statement of apology. The reporters then eagerly anticipated what Velma requested for her last meal. Initially, Velma just wanted the normally scheduled prison food; chicken livers, collard greens and a sheet cake with peanut butter icing. The last meal was delivered but Velma immediately lost her appetite. Instead, she opted for Cheese Doodles and a glass of Coca-Cola.

"Her attorney believed that Velma could have done some good in life," Orange said. "He stated that she could have become a teacher, counselor or a pastor. But her father set her on a path of self-destruction that she couldn't escape from. By the time she the left that road to ruin, she was too far gone in terms of her murderous acts. Justice had to be served in the end. In the end, the law doesn't care how genuine you are in your pleas for forgiveness. It only cares about the rule of law."

"I'm sorry for the hurt that I've caused," Velma said before her execution. "So many people, today if it were possible, I wish I could take every bit of hurt on myself."

BABY KILLER : THE TRUE STORY OF CHRISTINA MARIE RIGGS

19

DIANE ULLMER

Christina Riggs had all the drugs she needed.

She had filled her prescription for the anti-depressant Elavil at the pharmacy. She had stolen morphine and potassium chloride from the hospital. Now all she had to do was follow through.

"Kids," she bellowed out from the living room table. "Vitamins!"

The two sleepy-eyed children emerged from their bedroom. Christina gave them a small amount of Elavil, dropping the pill in their mouth and watching them drink it down with a cup of water.

A few minutes later, she carried them both back to bed.

Looking down at her two young children, she began to sob.

Shelby, just two years old, in her pink jumper. Justin, five years old, in his white pajamas with battleship designs.

I have to do this. Things will only get worse for them.

THE GREATEST TABOO

Christina Marie Riggs was twenty-six years when she decided to kill her children.

"A mother is supposed to protect her own children," Riggs' Defense Attorney John Wesley Hall Jr. said. "And here she didn't and it doesn't make sense. Two defenseless children that didn't know what was coming."

After Christina sedated her children, she proceeded with her plan of injecting them with potassium chloride. She knew that the drug was administered for lethal injection executions and would stop the heart within minutes.

What she didn't know was that the drug had to be administered in a diluted form. If it is injected without any dilution, it will burn through the skin then burst through the vein.

Ignorant of the consequences, Christina injected the lethal cocktail into her son Justin first.

She wanted a painless death. She did not want her children to go through life suffering like she did.

But then her son woke up screaming.

The potassium chloride she injected was binding and burning through his blood vessel linings.

He cried and cried and wouldn't stop.

Christina began crying herself...

CHILDHOOD TRAUMA

Christina Riggs had a troubled childhood growing up in Oklahoma City, OK.

She was separated from her brothers and sisters after her parent's divorce. Raised alone by her mother, she detailed in a prison diary sexual abuses that took place in her childhood.

She wrote how her stepbrother sexually abusing her from the age of seven to thirteen. At the age of thirteen, she was molested by a neighbor as well.

By the time she entered her teenage years, Christina was obese, using food as an emotional outlet. She also began abusing alcohol and marijuana.

"She indulged in overeating because she didn't want to appear attractive," forensic psychologist Paula Orange said. "That behavior was part of a psychological response to being molested. 'If I become fat and ugly then he won't want me anymore.' No one will bother me, no one will hurt me."

In her teenage years, however, Christina began to use sex as a way to get what she wanted, which was love.

"It isn't uncommon for abused young women to become very promiscuous," Orange said. "It is learned behavior. She became defective, if you will, and should have gotten help. Unfortunately, this is not a good recipe for someone who wants to have a healthy stable relationship and raise children."

"I felt that no boy liked me because of my weight," Christina wrote in her journal. "So I became sexually promiscuous because I thought that was the only way I could have a boyfriend."

She became pregnant by the age of sixteen but gave the baby boy up for adoption.

After high school, Christina went to a vocational school to become a licensed practical nurse (LPN). She obtained employment as a home care nurse and then later worked full-time at a VA hospital.

Her dating life remained steady albeit unsuccessful. She went from one man to the next, dating a Navy ensign named Jon Riggs and a bouncer before meeting Timothy Thompson. Thompson was an Air Force private at Tinker Air Force Base.

Three years after her first child, Christina would become pregnant with Timothy's baby. She informed Timothy her pregnancy the day before he was to be discharged from the Air Force.

Timothy, however, did not take the news well. He would not accept responsibility and moved back to his native Minnesota.

"Chrissy's luck with men was about zero to nothing," Carol Thomas, Christina's mother said.

But while her relationship ended with Timothy, Christina hooked back up with Jon Riggs who returned home after being on leave with the Navy.

"It was great," Christina wrote. "He felt the baby's first kick. As far as he was concerned, it was his baby."

Justin Thomas was born on June 7th, 1992.

"As I held Justin in my arms and looked into his little face, I became so scared," Christina wrote. "Would I be a good Mom? Could I give him all he needed?"

Riggs would move in with Christina and the two hoped for the best. Christina would become pregnant again and the couple would marry in July of 1993.

But misfortune would strike again as Christina would suffer a miscarriage on her wedding night.

The marriage would go south from there as Christina alternated between being depressed to having suicidal thoughts. She blamed her mental state on her birth control medication and a doctor gave her the anti-depressant Prozac.

The medication worked for a while but then Christina inexplicably stopped taking the drug. She kept her sadness to herself and didn't want to burden others with her problems.

"She's always been that way," Christina's mother said. "If I pushed her hard she might get mad and tell me what was going on."

By 1994, Christina would become pregnant and deliver a healthy baby girl in December named Shelby. This would mark the high point of Christina's life as "Sissie" and "Bubbie", the two nicknames for her children, brought immeasurable joy into her life.

She would write that it was the happiest time of her life as both she and Jon cried when they held their new baby in their arms. Things were happy for once in her life.

Christina continued to work as a vocational nurse and was assigned to work at a triage station which served to help the victims of the Oklahoma City Federal Building terrorist bombing. She would suffer post-traumatic stress disorder as a result. Later at her trial, the prosecuting attorneys would argue that the hospital had no record of Christina serving after the bombing. This may be nitpicking as authorities were lenient with record keeping during that urgent situation.

STRESS AND STRAIN

A year later, the couple would move to Sherwood, Arkansas to be closer to Christina's mother, Carole.

Carole worked as a food service worker at Baptist Hospital and Christina was able to find a job there as well, once again working as a licensed practical nurse.

The children go on to have ailments that would stress out the already fragile Christina. Shelby would have chronic ear infections that made doctor visits a routine thing. Justin was diagnosed with attention deficit disorder and his hyper nature would grate on the nerves of his parents.

Financial difficulties and the stress of running a family would put a strain on the marriage and the couple would eventually divorce. Her husband, Jon Riggs, had a volatile temper that he eventually took out on the young Justin. Jon would punch Justin in the abdomen with such force that the young boy had to go to the emergency room.

Jon would then abandon the family.

"Justin would say, 'My Daddy hurt me, and then he went away,' " Christina's mother recalled.

Christina would receive limited child support from Jon and had to work long hours to provide for her family. The more hours she worked, the more she had to pay for daycare which proved to be a daily traumatic event.

Shelby would cry as Christina would leave her at the facility.

"She was beating on the glass, yelling, 'Mama! Mama!' " Christina recalled.

Despite her increased efforts, Christina could not get ahead financially. She began writing bad checks. Bills remained unpaid. Car insurance. Car registration. Lights and utilities.

"I started out in a boat with a small hole," Christina said. "But the hole kept getting bigger, and no matter how hard you bail, you keep sinking. I was tired and I gave up. Suicide seemed like the only thing."

A HISTORY OF MENTAL ILLNESS

Christina had a cousin that killed herself. Her mother had also tried to kill herself when Christina was a baby. Her grandmother was committed to a mental institution.

But Christina would outdo them all in one fateful night.

"Just speaking in general," Orange said. "When mothers kill their children they do not poison them. In the case of Christina, she was applying what she thought would be a lethal injection."

But even with a history of mental illness in the family, nobody could have predicted how the sweet and caring Christina could commit such a heinous crime.

"Chrissy always wanted to help people," Christina's sister, Elizabeth Nottingham said. "She was always helping someone."

But Nottingham had some valuable psychological insight on her sister. She was a mental health counselor and had been close to Christina.

She wanted to know what drove her sister to kill her own children. After her sister's arrest, she began fishing around her house, looking for some kind of clue, a sign that everyone had missed.

"I was almost hoping to find that she wasn't a good parent," Nottingham said. "Then I could be mad at her. You know, I went through her house with a fine toothed comb. All the chemicals were locked away. The food was in the refrigerator. Even pictures of their fathers was in their room above each of their beds. She was great with the kids."

MORE TROUBLE WITH MEN

What Christina's sister would find out was that she simply could not find a decent man. That one relationship where everything would be ideal.

After her divorce from Jon, Christina would enter into another relationship which again would not go well.

"The guy didn't just break her heart," Nottingham said. "But took her credit card. I mean, it's one thing to have someone dump you, it's another to have someone rip you off and leave you destitute too."

After this break-up, Christina would sit at her dining room table both broke and broken-hearted. She had no man in her life. She had no means to pay her family's bills.

Seeing only dark lights ahead, Christina would lapse into a deep depression. She went to her doctor again who prescribed her more Prozac which used irregularly.

"She may have stopped taking the Prozac when she killed the babies," Orange said. "When someone just stops that medication cold-turkey it can have some side effects like increased irritability, irrational mood changes, and an even deeper depression."

"So she had the perfect storm brewing," Nottingham said. "She had depression, she had all of these personal failures. You know, people talk about having rainy days and Mondays. And in fact 'Rainy days and Mondays' was the CD that was in her CD player."

BACK TO THAT FATEFUL NIGHT

Christina had to kill herself. Her emotional bank account had been overdrawn for years.

But she couldn't stand the thought of leaving her children alone.

"If she left the kids behind," Hall Jnr said. "She was afraid that the children would be separated, go to their father's, for instance, and be split up."

"She just thought there was no other way out," Nottingham said. "She thought that no one else would take care of her kids. And that they would be better off, in her mind, she was saving them from future sadness."

With Justin screaming in pain, Christina panicked. She began sobbing but whatever remain of her maternal instinct kicked in and she tried to inject him with morphine.

Toxicology reports didn't reveal whether or not she did this.

But what she did do was suffocate her young son with a pillow. Sobbing, she then did the same deed to her baby daughter, Shelby.

Shaking with adrenaline and grief, Christina wobbled on shaky legs back to her living room. She took out her bottle of Elavil, an anti-depressant, and swallowed the remaining twenty-eight pills. Her nerves calming, she tried injecting the potassium chloride into her own arm.

The chemical burn right through her vein, collapsing it.

The drugs began taking effect and Christina fainted to the floor, hoping her nightmare would finally end.

THE DAY AFTER

The lethal mixture had burned a half-inch hole into Christina's arm. She didn't show up for work the next day and her mother called her cell phone and land line repeatedly.

Worried that she received no response, Carole drove to Christina's apartment and let herself in.

To her horror, she thought everyone was dead, including Christina.

"All I could do was turn around and around and scream and holler, 'No. No. No.' There's no way to describe how I felt."

Frantic, she called 911 and yelling into the phone, "My daughter and babies are dead."

Paramedics would arrive.

The children were dead.

But the medics were able to resuscitate Christina. She was transported to the intensive care unit and was kept under guard by the police.

"I had to do it so I wouldn't leave them behind," Christina was overheard saying in her hospital room. The treating physician, Dr. Jim Rice, would later testify that Christina as "combative at times" and "just incoherent and not really making any sense."

As soon as Christina became reasonably coherent, she was taken to the police station for booking.

THE INTERROGATION

On November 6th, 1997, Christina was interrogated by a Detective Jones and Detective Sharon Williams.

"Christina, what we are doing is investigating the death of your two babies. Do you want to tell us what happened?" Jones asked.

"I killed them," Christina said, crying.

"What did you say?"

"I said-"

"Did you say you killed them?"

"I'm sorry."

"How did you go about doing that?" Jones asked.

"I got some bottles and stuff from here...I need a cigarette...Darvocet."

"Are you saying that you got some medicine from the hospital?"

Christina nodded.

"Christina, how did you do it? Did you give them an injection? Did you give them a shot?"

"I tried to ... and ... I did it with Justin because I figured with him being the oldest one that he would give me more problems. So, I tried it with him and I thought it would just stop his heart. But it hurt. Oh, he said it hurt ...It didn't work, he just kept calling, 'Momma! Momma! Momma!' I just figured it was too late now because I had no place to turn back to. I cleaned out my checking account and gave my mother all the money I had."

"Christina, why did you do this?" Jones asked.

"Because I wanted to die," Christina said, crying again. "But I didn't want to die and leave my kids behind or for them to be a burden to somebody else. I didn't want them to think I didn't love them and I didn't want them to grow up separately because they have two different Daddies. And I knew if I passed away they would be fighting my Mother for custody and I didn't want that for nobody."

"You felt like you were doing it for the kids' sake?"

"In a way, yeah... my piece of mind."

"Christina, did you really want to die?"

Christina didn't respond. She continued crying.

"And you felt it would be better if your children just die with you and ... were the children already dead before you took your medicine?"

"Yes."

"How long had they been dead before you took your medicine?"

"About twenty minutes."

"About twenty minutes?"

"That's because I drank and got up and smoked a cigarette and got back and sit for a minute and...I was like, 'Okay, I'm going to do it now. I can't turn back now because you've already killed Justin.' And ... so I did it."

"What time did you give them the medicine? Do you remember?"

"Justin about 10:15 or 10:30."

"10:15 or 10:30 in the morning?"

"No, in the evening."

"Oh, in the evening?"

"Last night."

"Okay."

"Then I smoked another cigarette and waited," Christina paused. "And suffocated Shelby."

"You suffocated Shelby? What did ... how did you suffocate her?"

"I put a pillow over her head."

"Okay, Did you ... Had you given her any medicine at all, or ... any of the Morphine or the Potassium Chloride?"

"I slipped them ... I made them drink half of an Elavil because I figured that would make them sleep a little bit better so that it wouldn't wake them."

"So, Shelby, you killed her with a pillow. You suffocated her. And what about the little boy. How did you do him?"

"I gave him the medicine and when it didn't work."

"You suffocated him too?"

"Yes."

"With a pillow? Were they fighting while you suffocated them?"

"Justin did. Shelby a little bit but not much," Christina began to cry again.

"When did you decide to do this, Christina? On what day did you decide to do this?"

"Uh ... the best I remember it was Sunday night or Saturday night because we was out talking and this and that and the other ... and they caught me."

"Who caught you?"

"I was depressed. I was thinking about what was going on in my life and that things aren't always working for me and..."

"When did you get those drugs from the hospital?"

"When? Yesterday."

"Yesterday? You mean the day that you killed them? Is that the day that you got the drugs? The last was it ... "

"Was it the last day that you worked at the hospital or the day before that? "I think ...""

"When you got ... "

"I got the drugs and I gave them to my kids. That's the only drugs that I had in my hand. And I know that there was three Valiums in a vial in there, but there wasn't enough to even cover the jar up and put it in my pocket and bring them home. And I know I should have thought better ... had somebody rinsing with me, but ... they were just what came home in my pockets."

"Did you know what you were going to do when you took the drugs from the hospital? Did you have intentions of giving them to your children? And how many days did you think about this before you killed your children?"

"About three weeks. Two weeks."

"Two or three weeks. In other words, you've been thinking about doing this for the last two or three weeks? What made you decide to just go ahead and do it?"

"I just can't take it no more."

"You couldn't take it anymore."

"I felt like I was out of control," Christina said.

"Did you just feel like your life was in a mess? Had you talked to anybody about this? Your Mom or anybody?"

"I've tried to talk to people about what I feel and what I think and they were just like, 'I don't have time right now. We'll do it some other time.' So, I just got to where I don't care anymore. I tried but they can't give me no help."

"So you just felt like nobody was listening to you? Okay, Christina ...Christina, do you have anything more to say about your babies or anything? "I wish I hadn't done it now."

Christina would then go on an incoherent ramble, explaining how she saw her mother riding down an escalator with a bunch of old people. The detectives, however, got the damning evidence they needed and ended the interrogation.

PRISON AND JAIL

Christina would find a hostile environment in prison. The majority of her fellow prisoners were women who were taken away from their children by force. They had contempt for Christina's crime.

One inmate spat in her face and her life was threatened.

Christina was then moved to an isolated cell where she remained until her trial.

She would be charged with two counts of first-degree murder which was punishable by death in the state of Arkansas.

"We tried to show that she was under extreme emotional disturbance," Hall Jr said. "To justify either not imposing the death penalty or hopefully finding her guilty of second-degree murder."

"I just hope that out of all her misery," Nottingham said. "The sadness of our family. That we can shed some light on the causes of this for other people and that maybe they'll be able to look at the symptoms and look at the situations and maybe intervene for someone else."

But the prosecuting attorney, as well as the community, believed that Christina was guilty of performing a selfish act, an act wherein she tried to free herself from motherhood.

The most damning evidence at the trial, aside from the interrogation tapes, would be the account of the physicians.

One doctor would testify that it would take three to six minutes to suffocate someone to death. Because of that time period, the jurors would be able to envision how Christina commit a willful act of murder. Christina had, in essence, a struggling toddler under her pillow for about three to six minutes...suffocating to death.

"They just wanted her to be evil," Nottingham said of the prosecuting attorney's intent. "It was easier that way."

"Essentially, what the jury saw was that she was self-centered," argued Pulaski Prosecuting Attorney Larry Jegley. "That she viewed the children as an inconvenience and an interference with what she wanted to pursue. She placed her interests above those of the children."

Jegley argued that Christina was a self-centered and premeditated murderer. He brought up the fact that she had locked the children up in the house (according to a neighbor) in order that she could go out to a Karaoke party. He urged the jury not to buy into her manipulation to feel sorry for her. "There were lots of people who have it worse than she did."

The jury would side with the prosecution and find Christina guilty after a very short deliberation period.

THE IRONY

Christina Riggs would be sentenced to death by lethal injection via potassium chloride...The same method that she used to try to kill her children and herself.

"It was a cruel irony that they finished what she started," Hall Jr said. "Almost the exact same way except she was strapped down to a table."

Christina would appeal the sentencing but did so with reluctance.

She wanted to die.

"I'll be with my children and with God," Christina said. "I'll be where there's no more pain. Maybe I'll find some peace."

Her defense attorney John Wesley Hall Jr was allowed to witness the execution.

"You can see their face," Hall Jr said. "It allows them to say their last words. The face changes color as the drugs take effect. You turn gray. The skin turns gray. And it's rather shocking to watch it happen."

"She was so depressed that it became this black sheet over her eyes that she couldn't see through," Orange said. "She wanted to spare her own children from the kind of life that she had. She had lost complete hope and really over thought things. That's how her depression warped her. It warped her enough to think that she was doing her children a favor by killing them."

Christina was sent to death row and was haunted by the memories of her children. She openly stated that she tried "not to think about them" because when she did it was like someone "ripping them away from her all over again."

"A lot of regret," Christina said. "That's what goes through my mind, day-in, day-out. God's punishing me. He let me live so I would suffer."

Riggs was flown in from McPherson Jail to Cummins in order to prep for her execution. She would be administered the lethal injection at 9:28 PM CDT on May 2nd, 2000.

"No words can express just how sorry I am for taking the lives of my babies," Riggs said in a prepared statement. "No way I can make up for or take away the pain I have caused everyone who knew and loved them. I love you, my babies."

CHRISTA GAIL PIKE

paula buckley

34

Christa Gail Pike, born 10 March 1976, currently sits on Tennessee's death row for the murder of Colleen Slemmer, 19, on 12 January 1995. The murder occurred when Pike was 18 years old. Pike and her then-boyfriend Tadaryl Shipp who was 17 at the time of the murder were convicted of Slemmer's murder and conspiracy to commit murder. Another friend of the defendants and the victim, Shadolla Peterson, also 18 at the time, was convicted as an accessory after the fact and given six years' probation after turning informant. Pike was sentenced to death by electrocution in 1996 and, at the time, she had the distinction of being the youngest woman ever to be sentenced to death, in any state and only the second women given the death penalty in Tennessee.

Early Life

Pike's life reads like a primer for depraved murderers. As a small child, Pike did not enjoy a healthy and supportive bond with her mother, Carissa Hansen, a licensed nurse, allegedly because of her premature birth. Whereas thousands of children are born prematurely and do not resort to criminal behavior Pike's birth was presented as evidence of one possible origin of her poor and troubled behavior. Pike's maternal grandmother was verbally abusive and Pike was raised by her alcoholic and abusive paternal grandmother until the latter's death in 1988 when Pike was 12; after which Pike attempted suicide by overdosing. She was then shuttled back and forth between her divorced parents' homes. In 1989, Pike was kicked out of her father's house for the second and final time due to her unruliness and the alleged sexual abuse of her father's then-two-year old daughter with his second wife.

Prior to the murder, experts assert that there were myriad indications that Pike was seriously disturbed; however, nobody who may have suspected this sought help for the increasingly disobedient and incorrigible young lady. According to Pike's mother, she was problematic since the age of eight and the two of them had a contentious relationship due to Pike's fluctuating and troubling behavior. Her mother asserted that by age nine Pike was growing marijuana in pots at their home and had been permitted to have a live-in boyfriend at age 14. At one point—in an effort to improve their relationship—Hansen suggested that she and Pike smoke marijuana together. Hansen mistakenly believed that cultivating a friendship with her daughter would cultivate the necessary bond Pike had been lacking her entire life. At one point, one of her mother's boyfriends whipped Pike with a belt which prompted her to wield a butcher knife against him before he was subsequently arrested. Hansen also admitted that Pike had repeatedly lied to and stolen from her. In several interviews with Hansen throughout Pike's trial and seemingly endless appeals, she admitted repeatedly that she was a terrible mother and should have spent more time with her daughter.

Pike's aunt, Carrie Ross, provided insight into Pike's upbringing when she testified that she disallowed her own children from associating with Pike because she lived in a filthy house that had zero ground rules and that Pike was a pathological liar of whom she was somewhat afraid. She also admitted that there was a history of substance abuse in Pike's family. Ross also stated that on the few occasions that Pike actually visited her she behaved like a little girl and engaged in Barbie and dress-up play with her eleven-year-old cousin. Further, there were some allegations that Pike may have been sexually abused but these were neither confirmed nor denied.

Pike's father, Glenn Pike testified that he did, in fact, kick his daughter out of his house multiple times; the last time being in 1989 after the aforementioned allegations that Pike sexually abused her two-year old half-sister. He admitted that he had signed adoption papers for Pike prior to her 18th birthday and that during the times she resided with him she was manipulative, disobedient, and dishonest.

After dropping out of high school, Pike began Job Corps classes in computer programming. Job Corps is a government-based organization that provides occupational and vocational training to underprivileged and troubled teens. It was at the now-defunct Job Corps center in Knoxville where she met Shipp, Slemmer, and Peterson. While Job Corps seeks to promote prosocial behavior and foster a strong desire among its participants to learn a vocation and secure a more promising future than might have been previously the case, this program is also known to cultivate criminal activity, likely due to the association among its participants; many of whom already had problematic behavior.

Evidence of Premeditation

On 11 January 1995, the day before the actual homicide, Pike told friend and co-Job Corps student Kim Iloilo that she was planning to kill Slemmer because she "just felt mean that day." Iloilo discounted Pike's statement as nothing more than merely talk; however, the following evening at approximately 8:00 p.m. Iloilo witnessed Pike, Shipp, Peterson, and Slemmer leaving the Job Corps center. When Iloilo saw Pike, Shipp, and Peterson returning at approximately 10:15 p.m. without Slemmer she, again, thought nothing of it. Even when Pike visited Iloilo's dorm room at 11:00 p.m. that night and confessed to killing Slemmer—as well as showing Iloilo what Pike identified as a piece of Slemmer's skull—Iloilo still failed to tell anyone. Later, at Pike's trial, Iloilo testified that while Pike was iterating the events of the murder she was oddly smiling, singing, and dancing around the room. The following morning Iloilo asked Pike what she was going to do with the piece of skull. Pike nonchalantly replied that she had it in her pocket and was, in fact, eating breakfast with it.

Pike also told another student, Stephanie Wilson, a similar account the following day and proudly described the brown spots on her shoes as blood. Not unlike Iloilo, Wilson failed to immediately report anything.

The Crime Scene

On 13 January, officers from the University of Tennessee and Knoxville Police Departments were dispatched to greenhouses on the University's agricultural campus in Tyson Park where a University grounds department employee reported finding, at approximately 8:05 a.m., what he assumed to be a dead animal. The gruesome discovery was a corpse that turned out to be Colleen Slemmer. She was naked from the waist up; her throat was cut; her head had been bludgeoned; and she had various cuts all over her arms, throat, and torso—including a pentagram that had been carved into her chest. Officer John Terry Johnson who testified at Pike's trial described Slemmer's body as so badly beaten that she was unrecognizable as a human being. He also stated that he thought he was looking at her face when, in reality,

Slemmer was lying face-down in the dirt and debris where Pike, Shipp, and Peterson had left her.

There was additional evidence and testimony that the crime scene encompassed an area that measured 100 feet long by 60 feet wide; an astounding 6,000 square feet in area. Despite the area being muddy and wet there was ample evidence of a physical struggle with trampled bushes, a considerable amount of blood, body drag marks, and hand and knee prints. Thirty feet from Slemmer's body was a large pool of blood which suggested that Slemmer was attacked in one area and then dragged to where her body was later found. Slemmer's shirt and bra were also discovered at the crime scene, as well as a bloody rag that Pike admitted to tying over Slemmer's mouth at one point to keep her from screaming.

Disturbingly, University of Tennessee police officer Harold James Underwood, Jr., who was the officer assigned to secure the crime scene, testified at trial that Pike and a few other females came to the scene between four and five p.m. the day of the discovery and before Pike was even considered to be a suspect. Underwood stated that Pike had asked why the wooded area was marked off, who the victim was, and whether police had any leads as to who the suspect or suspects were. He particularly recalled Pike's odd behavior—moving around a lot while giggling amusedly—and that she wore a necklace in the shape of a pentagram. The following day, during briefing when informed that the victim had a pentagram carved into her chest, Underwood reported Pike's behavior and necklace to his supervisors.

Autopsy and Findings

During Slemmer's autopsy, the medical examiner, Dr. Sandra Elkins, had to identify the victim's body from dental records because her head was so bludgeoned that she was unrecognizable. After cleaning up Slemmer's body which was clad only in jeans, socks, and shoes, and covered with dirt and twigs, Dr. Elkins began cataloging Slemmer's wounds. Due to the sheer number of wounds on her back, arms, abdomen, and chest, and the fact that following department policy which stated that each individual wound be assigned a letter of the alphabet, when Dr. Elkins reached double letters she, instead, individually catalogued only the most serious wounds and that there were innumerable other superficial and defensive wounds. Among the most serious cuts was a six-inch gaping wound across Slemmer's throat that was deep enough to penetrate the fat and muscles in her neck as well as the aforementioned pentagram. Additional injuries included fresh bruising which Dr. Elkins asserted was consistent with crawling.

Cause of death was ultimately attributed to blunt force trauma to the head. Dr. Elkins surmised that Slemmer's head was hit with the asphalt at least four times—two to the left side, one over the right eye, and one to the nose—which collectively resulted in multiple and extensive skull fractures. One of these blows was to the left side of Slemmer's head—which, according to Dr. Elkins, occurred with the right side of the victim's head against a firm surface. This blow only fractured her skull but also imbedded a portion of Slemmer's skull into her head and contained black particles from the piece of asphalt determined to be the murder weapon.

Even more tragic was Dr. Elkins' findings that none of Slemmer's other wounds would have rendered her unconscious and evidence of active blood flow around the wounds and blood in her sinus cavity indicated that Slemmer was alive during the severe torture she suffered before being killed.

Arrest and Confession

The police quickly connected Pike to the homicide thanks to the piece of Slemmer's skull discovered in Pike's jacket pocket. Pike had left this jacket hanging on the back of a chair in Job Corps Orientation Specialist Robert A. Pollock's office on 13 January after meeting with him about a misplaced ID card. Pike's jacket remained in Pollock's office from 4:00 p.m. on 13 January until 7:30 a.m. on 17 January. After learning over the weekend that Pike was a suspect in Slemmer's murder investigation, Pollock immediately gave the jacket to William Hudson, the Job Corps' safety and security captain who turned it over to Knoxville Police Department Officer Arthur Bohanan. At trial, Bohanan would testify that he found a small piece of bone in one of the pockets and presented it to Dr. Murray Marks, a University of Tennessee forensic anthropologist who was reconstructing Slemmer's decapitated skull and the piece in Pike's jacket pocket fit perfectly into an area where a portion of her skull was missing at the time of the victim's discovery.

When confronted with this evidence and subsequently arrested, Pike waived her *Miranda* protections and confessed to the murder and permitted officers to search her dorm room where the blood-soaked jeans she wore the previous night were found. Additionally, Pike led officers to a trash can at a nearby Texaco station on Cumberland Avenue where she had disposed of Slemmer's ID and a pair of gloves Pike had been wearing at the time of the homicide.

Pike's transcribed confession was 46 pages long.

In it, Pike admitted that there was animosity between Slemmer and her because Pike was convinced that Slemmer was a rival for the affections of her boyfriend, Shipp, and that Slemmer was trying to get Pike kicked out of the Job Corps program so she could have Shipp for herself. Pike also claimed that she had awakened one night to find Slemmer standing above her with a box cutter; however, there is no evidence of this allegation. Instead, Slemmer had repeatedly called her mother, May Martinez, to tell her she was afraid of Pike who she had awakened to find in her room and that she wanted to come home; to which Slemmer's mother said that she couldn't because she had signed a contract. Pike stated that she had only planned to fight Slemmer to stop her from running her mouth. On that fateful night of 12 January, Pike, Slemmer, Shipp, and Peterson signed the Job Corps logbook as they were leaving for an outing Slemmer believed was to smoke marijuana en route to a video store so that Pike and she could try to work out their problems.

When the group entered a tunnel at the edge of Tyson Park, Slemmer likely felt that something was not quite right and proceeded to ask Pike where they were going and whether there was, in fact, any marijuana. These questions irritated Pike who began the brutal assault shortly thereafter after they had gone deeply enough into the woods so that nobody could hear them that led to Slemmer's murder.

Pike confessed to initially slamming Slemmer's head into her knee and then throwing her to the ground where Pike continually punched, kicked, and slammed Slemmer's head into the concrete, screaming, "the bi*ch won't die" and that she wanted "to see [Slemmer's] brains flow." According to witnesses Shipp and Peterson, as Slemmer continued to plead with Pike to stop, Pike got angrier and more brutal. Slemmer offered to return to her Florida home, leave her belongings at the Job Corps center, and not tell anyone what happened; however, Pike became more enraged and yelled at Slemmer to be quiet because "it was harder to hurt someone who was talking to you."

In addition to the savage beating, Slemmer had been cut innumerable times with a box cutter and a mini meat cleaver (that Pike had allegedly borrowed from another Job Corps student) to her torso, arms, face, and back including having had her throat slit six times prior to the fatal blow that resulted from having her head crushed by a piece of asphalt. There was also a pentagram carved into Slemmer's chest; however, Pike asserted that Shipp had done that. Pike also confessed to "just watching Slemmer bleed" when the victim got up and tried to run away. Pike admitted to cutting Slemmer's back: "the big long cut."

After the murder, Pike stated that she and Shipp washed their hands and shoes in a nearby mud puddle to conceal the blood, dumped the box cutter, and Pike returned the meat cleaver to the person from which she borrowed it. This person has never been identified.

The physical evidence and co-defendant testimony suggested that the assault and murder lasted from 30 minutes to an hour and consisted of Slemmer repeatedly trying to get up and run away but was prevented from doing so by the co-defendants who also, as Pike testified, contributed to the physical assault by throwing rocks at Slemmer's head and holding her down so she couldn't run away. Later, Pike would testify that she heard voices in her head overriding Slemmer's continual screaming, telling her that she needed to prevent Slemmer from filing charges against her for attempted murder. Pike also admitted that at one point she thought she had heard a noise and went to investigate it to ensure that they were alone, as well as alleging that during the assault she heard Slemmer breathing in blood and jerking but did not let this assuage her anger as Pike continued her savagery.

Even more troublesome, a police video recorded after Pike's confession shows Pike smiling and providing extensive details about the crime at the crime scene, oftentimes mimicking her actions that evening. Many have said that her demeanor on the recording was eerily similar to that of a little girl who was excited and happy that she had experienced the best day of her life and had no problem talking about the events that transpired, the heinousness of her actions, and how she felt about it all.

The facts of the homicide are not nor have they ever been in dispute, thanks to an abundance of evidence. Pike's confession, and witness testimony at the trial.

Pre-Trial Examination

Prior to her trial, Pike was given a battery of assessment tests and examined by numerous psychiatrists including clinical psychologist Dr. Eric Engum who found her to be extremely bright as evidenced by an I.Q. of 111—in the 77th percentile of the general population—which he believed to be remarkable given her difficult childhood and lack of formal schooling beyond the ninth grade. Dr. Engum also found that

Pike had excellent reasoning, problem solving, language, and analytic skills, and was also quite adept at paying attention, sustaining concentration, and sequencing information. Dr. Engum concluded that Pike was legally sane and had no brain damage which has frequently been demonstrated to cause violent behavior in some individuals.

Of particular interest was that Pike was found to be marijuana- and inhalant-dependent and also diagnosed with borderline personality disorder. Whereas there are some similarities between borderline personality disorder and antisocial personality disorder such as impulsivity, irritability, aggression, and a self-image that fluctuates between self-aggrandizement and despair, there are several differences. Individuals with borderline personality disorder differ from those with antisocial behavior in that the former—which primarily affects females—is characterized by a lack of remorse, self-destructiveness, black-and-white thinking, alcohol and/or drug use or abuse, unstable relationships characterized by fear of abandonment and extreme swings between love and hate, difficulty in achieving academic and vocational goals, and are more likely to have been sexually abused; while the latter—which affects disproportionately more males—is characterized by a lack of affect and remorse, emptiness, and an ultimate goal of self-preservation.

Pike demonstrated all of the aforementioned characteristics of borderline personality disorder which makes it easier—but not justifiably so—to comprehend how her intense jealousy of Slemmer and fear of losing Shipp made her commit her atrocious acts. In addition to her fear of abandonment, Pike also abused drugs, was likely sexually abused, had contentious relationships, and displayed zero remorse. Dr. Engum surmised that Pike did not act with premeditation or deliberation in Slemmer's murder but, instead, in a manner that was consistent with borderline personality disorder. More simply, Pike had lost control. However, on cross-examination Dr. Engum admitted that Pike's deliberate luring of Slemmer, that she carved a pentagram in the victim's chest, that she brought weapons with her, and that she bashed Slemmer's head into the concrete does, in fact, constitute deliberateness.

That Pike was overjoyed and singing in Iloilo's room describing the murder while dancing around with the portion of Slemmer's skull Pike had taken as a trophy further supported Dr. Engum's diagnosis of borderline personality disorder because she had eliminated who she perceived was in competition for her boyfriend, Shipp, and, therefore, could continue her relationship with him. When questioned about the piece of skull Pike had taken, Dr. Engum said that Pike had no identity and her actions of taking and displaying the skull was a way to get recognition, no matter how misleading and distorted said recognition might be. In fact, after her conviction and sentencing Pike wrote a letter to Shipp which was intercepted by jail personnel that stated that even though she tried to be "nice" to Slemmer by bashing in her head instead of letting her bleed to death she was still sentenced to "fry."

The Trial

There was an abundance of evidence presented at the trial. Physical evidence consisted of crime scene photographs, autopsy reports, bloody clothing, and the piece of Slemmer's skull Pike had taken as a trophy. With respect to this skull piece, Dr. Elkins presented Slemmer's decapitated skull that was reconstructed by Dr. Marks to explain the victim's injuries. The skull presented at trial was complete except for a portion that was missing on the left side of Slemmer's skull. Dr. Elkins demonstrated that the piece of skull found in Pike's jacket fit perfectly into this spot, much to the chagrin of Slemmer's mother who, in a taped interview, stated that Pike was oftentimes giggling and passing notes to her mother and defense attorney during the trial, not unlike an immature middle-schooler.

At the trial, the State introduced photographs taken of Pike and Shipp at the Knoxville Police Department in which both were wearing pentagram necklaces similar to the shape carved into Slemmer's chest. It was presented that both Pike and Shipp dabbled in devil worshiping and other forms of the occult and that Slemmer was a sacrifice for the next day, Friday the 13th. Despite the presence of some type of satanic elements in Slemmer's murder, Dr. William Bernet, Vanderbilt University's psychiatric hospital medical director, testified that the evidence was that of "an adolescent dabbling in Satanism." He further concluded that the concept of collective aggression—or mob mentality—in which a group of people become stimulated and subsequently engage in some type of violent behavior was most assuredly at play in the events leading to Slemmer's death. However, Dr. Bernet ultimately stated that he did not have enough evidence to definitively surmise whether Pike had acted with premeditation or intent when she lured and murdered Slemmer.

Pike was ultimately convicted of first-degree murder and conspiracy to commit first-degree murder after a mere two-and-a-half hours of jury deliberation. The fact that the jury returned guilty verdicts for first-degree murder—and did it so quickly—demonstrate that jurors were convinced that Pike had the requisite mens rea, or mental capacity, to warrant a first-degree murder charge: premeditation and deliberation. Amidst the overwhelming evidence and utter lack of remorse for her actions Pike was sentenced to death by electrocution (Tennessee has since adopted lethal injection for executions but has the prerogative to utilize electrocution if the lethal injection drugs cannot be obtained). Shipp was sentenced to life without parole because his age at the time of the murder was too young to warrant capital punishment and Peterson turned informant and was given six years' probation for her testimony.

Pike's conviction was upheld by the Court of Criminal Appeals and the United States Supreme Court denied certiorari.

Post-Conviction

While incarcerated, Pike demonstrated more evidence of her depravity. In 2001 she tried to murder fellow inmate Patricia Jones by strangling her with a shoelace. Pike alleges that Jones repeatedly tortured her by calling her "fried chicken" and making various demeaning sounds as an affront to what Jones said was the sound that Pike would make when she was electrocuted. The final straw was when Jones physically threatened Pike's friend, fellow devil worshiper Natasha Cornet. Pike said that she jumped atop Jones and choked her with a shoelace so that the much larger and heavier Jones would get off of Cornet. By the time prison guards reached them, Jones was unconscious.

Pike was subsequently convicted of attempted murder despite her prior death sentence because any offense committed while an individual is incarcerated must be adjudicated. During this time, neurology specialist Dr. Jonathan Henry Pincus began investigating Pike's brain to glean some type of knowledge as to why Pike behaved and continued to act violently the way she did when she assaulted Jones. He asserted that every killer he has ever examined share three commonalities: brain damage, a history of abuse, and mental illness. Dr. Pincus alleged that Pike did, in fact, possess all three features and demonstrates all of the requisite features common to serial killers. There is much consensus among professionals that Pike would likely have been a serial killer had she not been caught the first time.

He also testified at Pike's attempted murder trial that her brain's frontal lobes are not "put together properly"; largely due, he claimed, to the fact that Pike's mother drank while she was pregnant with Pike despite denial of this by Pike's mother. It was also brought up that as a child Pike played at the slaughterhouse where her grandfather worked and that she was frequently subjected to pornography and horror movies on the home television screen. He asserted that all of these factors provide insight into how an 18-year old girl could act with such depravity as was the case when Pike murdered Slemmer.

However, the original trial judge, Mary Beth Leibowitz, stated that Pincus' "findings" of brain damage was curious as the defense expert at Pike's original trial who was trying to spare her the death penalty failed to find such evidence.

Forensic psychiatrist William Kenner testified that Pike had suffered from undiagnosed bipolar disorder, the symptoms of which were evident from the time Pike was a "sleepless, talkative adolescent" and likened her to an automobile with cruise control set at 120 miles per hour. Pike's post-conviction defense team alleged that this non-diagnosis justified her requesting a new trial.

In 2002 Pike sought to have her appeal legally stopped and to proceed with her execution. In June of that year Judge Leibowitz granted Pike's request and scheduled an execution date of 19 August 2002. However, a few days later Pike changed her mind and the Tennessee Court of Appeals subsequently stayed her execution. In October 2005, Pike's death sentence was affirmed; however, no execution date has been set at this time.

Pike was again in court in 2007 when her defense team headed by Donald E. Dawson asserted sought a new trial, alleging ineffective assistance of counsel in that her trial defense team failed to introduce evidence supporting Pike's alleged bipolar disorder. During this hearing, Shipp admitted to misinforming investigators and that he, in fact, was primarily responsible for Slemmer's murder. He stated that he was drunk and tired and just wanted the police to leave him alone when he put the onus of blame on Pike. Additional testimony from prior Job Corps student and the defendants' mutual friend Tyrone Comfort stated that Shipp controlled and abused Pike despite her assertions that he was the first male to protect her and she admired the respect and fear he elicited from others. Pike, however, was heavily medicated during this hearing for her alleged bipolar condition and the hearing was rescheduled for April 2008.

During her 2008 hearing, prosecutors portrayed Pike as a cold-blooded vicious killer who not only planned Slemmer's murder but prolonged it for sport, essentially playing cat-and-mouse with Slemmer by allowing her to get up and try to escape and then pushing her back on the ground for additional torture. Ultimately, her request for a new trial was denied.

Pike became newsworthy again in 2012 when she formulated an escape plan with the help of 34-year-old New Jersey resident Donald Kohut who frequently visited Pike in prison but the extent of their relationship remains unknown, and 23-year-old former prison guard Justin Heflin. In a joint investigation by the Tennessee Department of Corrections, the Tennessee Bureau of Investigation, and the New Jersey State Police after receiving information about the plan, both men were arrested and charged with bribery and conspiracy to commit escape, with Heflin charged with an additional facilitation to commit escape charge due to his job as a prison guard. Authorities discovered contraband evidence in the facility which could have only been brought in by a staff member and that Heflin was likely involved. Further investigation demonstrated that Heflin knew Kohut and that Heflin was receiving gifts and money for his assistance in the escape plan. Pike was also charged.

Even more recently, during yet another post-conviction relief hearing in 2015, testimony revealed that Pike was allegedly pregnant at the time of the murder. While this may be true it neither excuses her actions nor provides any potential evidence of legal insanity to justify an affirmative defense of not guilty by reason of mental disease or defect or guilty but mentally ill. Also during this hearing, Slemmer's mother requested the missing piece of her daughter's skull so she could bury the whole of her daughter but was denied as the skull piece remains a critical piece of evidence in Pike's ongoing legal appeals.

Since exhausting the state appeal process, Pike's new defense attorney, Assistant Federal Defender Stephen A. Ferrell, filed a

123-page petition on her behalf alleging that he constitutional rights were violated in both the original 1996 trial and penalty phase and that Tennessee's appellate courts ignored said violations. Among these claims is that capital punishment would amount to cruel and unusual punishment in violation of the Eighth Amendment of the United States Constitution because of Pike's youth, immaturity and mental illness. While Shipp—only 17 at the time of the murder—was too young to warrant imposition of a death sentence, Pike was not. Ferrell alleged that her trial lawyers were incompetent and failed to introduce evidence of mental illness, brain injury, and post-traumatic stress disorder. In response, the state Attorney General submitted a 90-page rebuttal repeatedly asserting that the state courts' ruling were all legally correct. As of the beginning of 2016, this battle continues.

Numerous video interviews of Pike over the past several years show her admitting that she was fully cognizant of her actions and that they were wrong. She stated that she felt as though she was taking out years of abuse on Slemmer and that she committed a horrible atrocity and deserves to be punished; however, she asserts that she deserves life without the possibility of parole for her actions; not the death penalty for the actions of three individuals. She has repeatedly stated that she wishes it was she who died and not Slemmer but such protestations are moot after the fact. One cannot help but wonder if Pike actually means what she says or is simply saying what she thinks others want to her. Knoxville Police Department detective Randy York who worked the case has said that in his lengthy career he has not encountered many people who he believes are evil but that Pike is, indeed, the personification of evil and that she should never be permitted to be around other human beings ever again.

Experts assert that the death penalty is not an effective general deterrent and debate over the morality and legality of capital punishment remains contentious and in the forefront of public discourse and debate. Currently, Tennessee is only one of 38 states which have the death penalty. Whereas women comprise 13% of those arrested for murder, only 2% are sentenced to death and, of those, only 3% are actually executed; primarily due to judges not wanting to sentence women to death. In Tennessee, only two individuals on death row have been executed—both males. The last time a woman was executed in the state was in 1837. Many currently believe that Pike will likely never be executed.

KILLER RETARD: THE TRUE STORY OF BRANDY HOLMES

RHONDA NORMAN

It was New Year's Day in 2003 when retired pastor Julian Brandon heard a knock on his door in Blanchard, Louisiana. He opened it to find the villainous duo of Brandy Holmes and Robert Coleman who "bum rushed" the 70-year old man, forcing their way in.

The couple shot the minister and began ransacking his home.

His wife, Alice, tried hiding in the back bedroom but Brandy and Coleman followed her, demanding valuables before shooting her.

They then stole whatever they could out of the home; cash, credit cards, and jewelry.

Brandy would only be captured after she bragged to one of her neighbors that she killed an elderly couple.

She would be sentenced to death but would blame being born with fetal alcohol syndrome for her behavior. By doing this, she could avoid personal responsibility, as her life was filled with murder and mayhem.

"I was named after my mother's favorite drink," she said. "Brandy."

Born out of a childhood of neglect and growing anger, Brandy Holmes would become one of the most vicious killers in Louisiana history.

EARLY LIFE

Brandy's mother, Brenda Bruce, would drink whiskey through the first three months of her pregnancy before switching to beer. She would give birth to Brenda Aileen Holmes on July 25th, 1979 in Tylertown,

Mississippi.

Brenda and her common-law husband Johnny Holmes would separate
early in Brandy's life, however. Brenda would then take the two-year-
old Brandy and leave for Shreveport, Louisiana. Brandy would be
neglected by Brenda throughout her younger years as her mother
would battle her own alcoholism addiction as well as having to deal
with two other children from a previous union.

As the product of a neglectful home, Brandy began acting out. This
would not be documented until she entered elementary school where
she became an immediate discipline problem. Inside the school, she
yelled at teachers, ate rocks in the schoolyard and was soon placed into
special education classes. Her out of control behavior would not be
limited to school as one day when she returned home, she killed a
kitten.

**At the age of twelve, Brenda would claim that Brandy was raped.
She would then be institutionalized at Sand Hill Hospital in
Mississippi for six months. Psychiatrists would later state that
Brandy had the mental function of a seventh grader and had no
empathy for other people.**

**She would drop out of school in the sixth grade. By the age of
thirteen, Brandy was running with a "black street gang" and
participated in drive-by shootings. She would be expelled from
school after bringing knives to class.**

Now free from academic obligations, Brandy would embark on a
crime career full-time, committing small-time thefts and home
burglaries. On one occasion, she and a boyfriend tried to kidnap a girl
in Mississippi in the hopes of holding her for ransom. In and out of

juvenile hall, her disdain for authority would manifest itself in numerous occasions as she fought with corrections officers. In one instance, she got a hold of a piece of broken glass and cut the throat of one of the officers.

"Brandy had a pathological dislike for anyone in authority," forensic psychiatrist Gil White said. "She had spent her entire life in and out of juvenile hall. This would mean daily encounters with fellow inmates who were just as evil and malicious as she was. But she always made it a point to do them one better. There was one inmate who would taunt Brandy at the corrections facility on a daily basis. Brandy knew that her harasser would come at her at only certain times during the day. So she got a bottle of acid and waited for the girl to come into her cell. The taunts began and Brandy threw the acid into the young woman's face. Her victim screamed as the acid burned into her eyes and face. Brandy would only laugh in satisfaction."

Brandy would be continuously incarcerated for most of her life, never holding a job. She had an IQ of 77 but still plotted out elaborate burglaries, knowing how to "police" herself afterward by not leaving behind fingerprints or evidence.

"Brandy talked as if she were 'black'," White said. "She mimicked the voice and cadence of someone who grew up in a black ghetto. The majority of her friends were black and she embraced the culture of ghetto crime early on. She loved committing crimes and then bragging about them to anyone who would listen."

She would break and enter homes until her another arrest got her a juvenile prison sentence for six years until she turned twenty-one. Once again, she would fight correctional officers at the Jetson Correctional Center for youth and would be sentenced as an adult

to the Louisiana Correctional Institute for Women.

"Brandy's reputation around the jail had reached the warden," White said. "The warden would comment on how she had been unable to break down Brandy. That is how incorrigible she was. Her behavior had stood out to someone who had seen everything over a period of decades. But the one person she would single out as being 'tough' was Brandy Holmes."

She would be released at the age of twenty-three but only more mayhem would await. She had remained out of jail for over seven months but her criminal mind started to each. Brandy began to think bigger in terms of obtaining that adrenaline rush in committing a crime.

GETTING BOLDER

During Christmas Eve of 2002, Brandy would visit her father Johnny in Tylertown, Mississippi. He lived near the dubious "Cloud Nine" neighborhood which was one of the most violent-prone in the state. It was a biracial community with a lot of drugs and shootings among the numerous mobile homes.

Brandy felt right at home in the "Cloud Nine" neighborhood as she visited her father's trailer on the pretense of a visit. But what she really wanted was his gun.

She watched as her father shot the gun off during a celebration and noted where he kept the weapon for safekeeping.

When he wasn't looking, Brandy took the .380 caliber handgun and returned to Louisiana.

She hooked up with her boyfriend, Robert Coleman upon arriving back home. Coleman was an African-American man with a long history of criminal behavior. He walked with a perpetual scowl and victimized people of all skin colors.

"Robert was ten years older than Brandy," White said. "She saw him as a kind of hero as he did things she always wanted to do but didn't have the muscle or nerve."

They became a crime duo, robbing other gang members and committing petty thefts.

Now armed with a .380 caliber gun, Brandy got a little bolder than usual.

During a New Year's celebration at her mother's home, Brenda asked everyone what their New Year's resolution was. Without hesitation, Brandy pulled out the gun from her purse.

"I'm about to 'hit a lick.'" Brandy said, kissing Coleman.

"Hitting or jacking a lick," White said. "Meant that she was going to commit a crime of some sort. Probably a robbery. But everyone at the party was probably so drunk or high they didn't care."

Robert Coleman, however, took Brandy seriously. He saw the gun as a tool for them to commit more crimes.

"That's why she was drawn to Robert," White said. "He was described by one detective as one of the most callous human beings she had ever encountered. That's what drew Brandy to him. Plus, he accepted her in ways that the upstanding young men in the community didn't. Brandy was overweight with a bulbous forehead and a mean facial expression. Her potential suitors were not church-going college students. Her suitors, and she didn't have a lot, were bad people. Men like Robert Coleman."

LET THE STALKING BEGIN

Looking for people to rob, Brandy would enter a gated community called "Nob Hill", a place for elderly residents. Seemingly picking out a house at random, Brandy knocked on the door of Patricia Camp.

"Hi there," she said. "Is Theresa McGee here?"

"I'm sorry," Camp said. "There's no one here by that name."

Thinking she had an easy target, Brandy enlisted the aid of her boyfriend Robert Coleman and returned to Camp's residence. The two knocked on the door and Brandy asked if she could use the phone.

Now suspicious, Camp refused and closed the door.

If she had let the duo into her home she would have robbed and most likely murdered.

A VICTIM BY CHANCE

On New Years Day, Brandy decided that she would visit the grave of a friend in a rural town called Blanchard.

Blanchard was a relatively peaceful and quiet rural area with a population of less than 3,000. Violent robberies and murders simply did not happen there.

Until Brandy Holmes decided to pay a visit.

While mourning over her friend's gravestone, she noticed an elderly couple that lived behind the graveyard. Brandy watched from behind the headstones as the married man and wife performed their gardening duties.

They were old. They were vulnerable. They probably had money considering they had the biggest house in the neighborhood.

They were the Julian and Alice Brandon, known to most everyone in town as the nicest people around town. People who would give you the shirt off their back.

"They were well-loved at church and in the community," White said. "They were getting ready to celebrate their fiftieth wedding anniversary."

Brandy then contacted her partner in crime, Robert Coleman, and told him of the couple she had spotted near the graveyard.

"Time to hit a lick," she told Coleman when she came home. "I found the perfect couple. They are as weak as kittens!"

This go around, Brandy made a necessary adjustment to her ruse. She would not make the same mistake she did with Patricia Camp by being too polite. This time, she would not use the pretense of looking for a person who didn't live there or ask to use the telephone.

She would use Coleman's muscle to force their way inside.

Lounging around their home in the early evening, Julian and Alice sipped hot cocoa while watching a television program.

Then came a knock at the door. They weren't expecting anyone this late in the evening and Alice looked concerned.

"I'll see who it is," Julian got up and went to the door.

Opening up, he was forced out back into the home by the gun-toting Robert Coleman.

Brandy barged in and watched as Coleman placed the handgun under the Pastor's jaw and fired.

The bullet separated into two pieces, one fragment entered his brain while the other exited the top of his head and into the dining room ceiling.

Blood splattered on the wall as Pastor Julian fell to the ground.

Brandy and Coleman then grabbed Alice. They dragged her to the back bedroom and demanded everything she had. Cash, credit cards, and jewelry.

"Brandy and Coleman were devils," White said. "Monsters. They shot Julian almost immediately upon entering the home. Alice didn't know what to do. It was like a nightmare come to life. They grabbed her and demanded credit cards. ATM cards. They demanded to know the PIN numbers."

The 68-year old woman begged for her life but the two demons would not hear it.

"Oh, Sweet Jesus!" Alice screamed. "Oh, Sweet Jesus, please don't shoot me!"

Alice's hysterics made Brandy anxious. The monster then placed a pillow over the elderly woman's head and ordered Coleman to shoot her.

They returned to the dining room and to their amazement, saw the Reverend Julian struggling to get up.

Brandy then went to the kitchen and found three Chicago Cutlery knives in the drawer. She and Coleman then began stabbing the Reverend to death. They would slice at his nose and face then stab him in his head and chest.

"They were each trying to upstage the other," White said. "Brandy was trying to show Robert what a 'bad ass' she was by stabbing the old man. He, in turn, enjoyed the admiration he received from Brandy. He liked doing 'evil shit' in order to gain her worship."

They would then cut the Reverend's throat two times, a slicing would that encircled his entire neck, severing his carotid artery and jugular vein.

Brandy then left one of the knives embedded in Pastor Julian's back, six-inches deep.

Their handiwork done, Brandy "policed" the place, wiping for fingerprints as well as removing the bullet casings from the floor and the ceiling. But it was all futile as the two left bloody footprints all over the house.

Brandy would then take the Reverend's ATM card and try to withdraw cash. When that failed, Brandy burned the card and tossed it in the woods behind her mother's trailer along with the gun.

She then tried to pawn off the jewelry to a neighbor. The neighbor described Brandy as taking pleasure in showing him the wedding rings, gold bracelets, and other valuables. He then asked where she got all of the jewelry and she bragged "I killed some old people.

The neighbor scoffed at the answer which seemed to make the insecure Brandy angry. She wanted to be seen as a 'bad ass'.

Two days later, Brandy would take her nephews to the Brandon residence. She would enter the home with one of her nephews (a 9-year old) and upon making too much noise in the house they would hear Alice screaming for help in the back bedroom. Both of her nephews would sprint away from the residence while Brandy would remain in the home.

MORE MAYHEM

Wanting that same adrenaline high, the couple would seek out a gang member friend named Terrance Blaze. Blaze would get inside their vehicle in the front passenger side seat with Coleman driving. Brandy, sitting in the backseat, would shoot Blaze in the head at point-blank range. They would then dump the body near her mother's trailer.

"Blaze was a friend of theirs," White said. "He was twenty-five years old. They killed him simply for the thrill of it. There was no motive involved in the killing of Terrance Blaze. This was a case of them not wanting to experience the same high of killing the Brandon couple.

They had to kill again and Terrance was a convenient target."

THE DISCOVERY

The brutalized couple would not be found until January 5th, 2003, four days later. Calvin Hudson was a family friend of the Brandons and became concerned when the couple did not come to church that Sunday. He went to check on them and found Pastor Julian lying in a pool of his own blood on the carpet. Panicked, Hudson went to a neighbor's home and police were called.

Amazingly, they discovered that Alice Brandon was still alive. Medical personnel was called and they arranged for a helicopter to come and medivac Alice to the hospital as the house was in a rural part of the parish.

The details of the horrific crime made the news and the Caddo Parish Sheriff's Office would receive tips from people who lived at an apartment complex near the Brandon residence. One of them included the man whom Brandy tried to sell off Alice's jewelry.

Obtaining their identification, police converged on the trailer of Brandy's mother, Brenda Bruce. Inside, they would find Brandy, Coleman and Brandy's 15-year-old brother, Sean George.

Inside the trailer, investigators would find a multi-colored bracelet that belonged to Alice Brandon. A box of food service gloves were found which had a diamond pattern consistent with the blood transfer stains found at the murder scene. Also, three fired .380 cartridge casings were found in the gutter of the trailer. These casings would later much the casings found on Brandy's father's property when he had fired the gun into a tree prior to it being stolen.

THE INTERROGATION

The detectives found Brandy to be a willing informant after some initial resistance. They had her remove her shoes as they knew it would match the bloody footprints they found at the Brandon residence. Brandy knew she had been caught dead to rights and she also couldn't resist the opportunity to tell the detectives about her crimes.

"I can show you where I threw their credit cards," she said. "But then I'd have to show you something else. A dead body. "

She was informed of her Miranda rights and told them about the body of Terrance Blaze without any prompting.

"Brandy came from a prison culture where everyone got an ego boost as they talked about the crimes they committed," White said. "The more horrific the crime, the bigger the rep. So Brandy could not resist the ego boost that she thought she could get by telling the detective about her crimes, in essence, she was bragging about them to the interrogator. Her need to feel validated trumped her need to not incriminate herself."

The detective then put his guard down and left Brandy alone at the desk. She realized that the videotape recorder had filmed her entire confession. Seizing the opportunity, Brandy took the tape from inside the camera and replaced it with a blank one she found on the detective's desk. He returned and she asked to go to the bathroom. She then flushed the tape down the toilet.

Police would discover the ruse and were still able to prosecute Brandy without her taped confession.

While incarcerated, Brandy did not take the whole process seriously. Her attorneys noted that she didn't seem to fully understand the extent of the punishment she was about to receive. Her letter to a friend after her arrest reflects her mindset at the time.

"Hey Chaz,

I know you thought I forgot about you. No Never that Honey. I'm Back locked up if you didn't see it on the news or in the newspaper. Girl, yes. They got me charged with 1st degree murder armed robbery attempted 1 st degree murder and 2nd degree murder. I sit there and watched my Baby's Daddy kill these white folks and yes I took the Visa card the gold Mastercard and the codes and cleaned there Bank accounts out. They was going to Book my 15 year old Brother, But I went ahead and took all charges & I have Affidavit to get notarized so I can let my Baby's daddy go to[o]. You know damn well I'm going to try my Best to escape and you know this too. I got it mostly planned. Don't be mad, Chaz. I gotta have my Money ya know. I goes back to court Feb. 18th 03 Girl don't worry yourself about me. I'll be okay, I guess you know. You be cool and write me back and tell me the low down/who all is Back up in there okay.

Here's my address okay .

Love Always,Ms. Brandy"

Her letter above was admitted as evidence. It would be used to show that Brandy had forethought when she committed her crimes.

"But for Brandy and Robert meeting each other, they both would have probably been limited to burglaries and incarceration," White said.

"But the both of them together was like a match to dynamite. The crimes would have escalated and they would have hurt a lot of people."

Alice Brandon, the lone survivor of Brandy's rampage, would be comatose for several years before finally passing away in October of 2008. Alice would be disabled for the rest of his life and required the insertion of feeding and tracheotomy tubes.

In 2005, both Coleman and Brandy would be convicted of first-degree murder. Brandy is one of only two women who are on Louisiana's death row.

SO DAMN EVIL

GERALDINE PAGE

Louise Melanie "Louise" May was looking for a place to stay.

She had three children but had them taken away as the courts declared her to be an unfit parent because of her drug addiction. At the age of 23, she needed to get her life back together.

Things seemingly could not get any worse for the recovering addict.

But then she arrived at the home of Kerry Dalton seeking help.

"I don't have anywhere to go," Louise said, realizing that her audience in Kerry Lyn Dalton was only half paying attention. "Rob is in jail. They took away my kids. Damn CPS."

The frazzled haired twenty-eight-year-old alternated between staring at the television and smoking on the meth pipe. She took a deep toke on the pipe and let the smoke out.

"You can stay with me," she finally said.

"Oh my God, thank you," Louise said.

"But it is only until Rob gets out," Kerry said.

"I understand. I understand. No problem."

But Louise had a problem. Meth addiction.

Now she had added another problem in Kerry Lyn Dalton.

"Kerry was a queen in the subculture of meth and alcoholism if there is such a thing," forensic psychologist Greta Smith said. "She had been married twice and had five children by three different men. It was amazing how Kerry Dalton even survived to the age of 28. Unemployable, she was the epitome of a bully and would do anything to get her way. She had little regard for the rights or feelings of other people, running roughshod over everyone in her path."

Unfortunately for Louise, she had gotten in Kerry's way.

Kerry would be arrested for drug possession and hauled off to jail for a short stint. She had been Louise's supplier and Louise needed her fix.

But she had no money.

So she began pawning off things she found around the house during a spur of the moment "garage sales." Some of Kerry's old jewelry would be sold off in exchange for drugs.

But when Kerry was released from prison and found out that her stuff had been pawned off, she became more than livid.

She became homicidal.

"Kerry took the theft as a personal affront," Smith said. "This was a fragile living situation between two drug addicts. Junkies. They had little regard for one another and really see each other as utilities to use or supply drugs. Louise is willing to sell out Kerry's stuff while Kerry is willing to kill Louise to gain revenge."

On June 26th, 1988, Kerry confronted Louise at the mobile home. Three other people in their drug dealing clique soon arrived, Mark Lee Tompkins, Sheryl Baker and another transient named "George".

Kerry ordered Louise to sit down and tied her to a chair. She then began torturing her, splicing off and electrical cord and burning her with it.

Louise screamed in pain.

Tompkins then began joining in the torture, jabbing at the defenseless Louise with a screwdriver.

The two then demanded that Sheryl partake in the abuse as well. Reluctantly, Sheryl complied.

"Sheryl felt as if they would have killed her if she didn't do as she was told," Smith said.

After the course of a few hours, the three then took turns torturing Louise.

Kerry enjoyed shocking her captive with the electric cord, laughing as Louise screamed. Seeking to raise the stakes, her boyfriend took an iron skillet and smashed it against the back of Louise's head.

"They hit her with such force that it made a dent in the pan," Smith said.

Kerry's sadism was still not satiated. She kept thinking of different ways to torture Louise then came up with the idea to inject her with some battery acid. Her boyfriend got a syringe and they plunged the battery acid into her vein as well as poured it down her throat.

"Kerry was a sadist," Smith said. "She justified her torture of Louise to the fact that the woman sold a few items of her jewelry and got maybe twenty-five bucks for it."

Tompkins then put Louise out of her misery by stabbing her in the neck with the screwdriver. She fell to the ground and he began stomping on her head until she died.

What happened to Louise's body after remains shrouded in mystery and hearsay.

Later that evening, a sheriff arrived at the mobile home on a burglary call. He saw no evidence of a burglary but did describe one of the residents, Joann Fedor, as high on meth. The sheriff then inspected the exterior and interior of the mobile home, finding nothing.

The disappearance of Louise remained unsolved for three years until Sheryl Baker had a crisis of conscience. She confessed to the crime, telling the authorities of what happened the day Louise was killed. In return for her confession, the authorities allowed her to plead to second-degree murder.

One of Louise's cousins stated on-line that the prosecuting attorney told her that one of trio involved admitted that they dismembered the body of Louise. They then spread the body parts out across different locations on different Indian reservations.

"For meth heads," Smith said. "They certainly knew what they were doing when disposing of a body. They were all jobless junkies but when it came to murdering someone they were willing to work hard. Damn hard in order to avoid detection. They would have avoided detection but for Sheryl Baker finally coming forward."

Kerry's trial would begin on February 8th, 1995. The judge, Thomas J. Whelan stated that

"I think the record is clear that nobody has ever been found in this case. The record is equally clear that there is circumstantial evidence that there was a homicide. There's also conflicting circumstantial evidence that it may not be a homicide; in fact, she may still be alive ..."

"My reason for making these statements is to establish for the record that in my mind corpus is a legitimate issue in this case. It's not a ruse that - there is a legitimate issue before the jury as to whether or not there's - a corpus of a homicide has been established."

Kerry would never confess to the crime on record and would claim innocence.

"The thing that makes me the most mad is that he is lying, and he knows he's lying," Kerry said of the prosecuting attorney.

The jury foreman, John Castleman, would concede that they found her guilty on the basis of "the type of murder it was" despite a lack of physical evidence to prove that Louise was murdered.

Mark Thompkins would be convicted of first-degree murder.

Kerry Dalton would be sentenced to death on May 23rd, 1995.

"She is the epitome of evil," Smith said. "We can say the drugs did it but there was a lot of premeditation to what she did to poor Louise. If anyone deserves to be on death row and have her execution expedited, it is Kerry Dalton."

Victoria Forbes, however, continues to champion the innocence of her sister.

"She was convicted without a body," Forbes said. "Without a weapon, without any blood evidence, without any physical evidence, without a crime scene, without anyone being declared deceased nearly seven years later as she stood trial with no one declared deceased being charged with the death penalty."

There continued to be some on-line controversy regarding Kerry's guilt as her supporters point to the fact that Louise's husband claims to have had a call from Louise a week after she was murdered.

That "evidence", however, is all they have to go on.

Despite Dalton's persistence at an appeal, it was clear to law officials believe that Kerry Dalton was guilty of the murder of Irene Louise May. Neither Tompkins nor Baker had anything to go after coming forward after three years of silence. They finally sobered up and confessed their crime.

Kerry Dalton did not and is now on death row.

SHEILA LABARRE

PROLOGUE

The farmhouse and surrounding area looked like something from the set of "Little House on the Prairie."

The house on Harvey Farm stood nestled in between tall pine trees, peaceful streams, and wildlife.

A place where you don't expect to find scenes that would be given an "X" rating if it were a horror movie.

The police arrived at the home while conducting a search for a missing young man named Kenneth Countje. They did not have to search far to find evidence of criminal activity. In the front of the property, lay a mattress burning alongside a smoking garbage barrel.

Their first inclination was to believe that the resident was burning garbage. A citation was due, maybe, but they had more pressing matters to attend to.

But upon closer inspection of the barrel, the officers saw a bone sticking out of the garbage.

A femur?

A mass of fleshy goo remained at the knob of the bone and the smell of the charred remains made the policemen gag.

They both gave each other a look of horror. Here in a town where the most serious crime would be a speeding ticket or jaywalking, the police were about to enter a whole world of horror beyond their wildest imagination.

CHAPTER ONE

Epping, New Hampshire.

Population = less than six thousand.

Epping is a rainy, small town that has been sarcastically nicknamed "The Center of the Universe". That has not stopped the residents from hosting parades, canoe races and music festivals. But when Sheila LaBarre arrived, the tiny hamlet soon became known for murder.

"She was a smart woman," forensic psychologist Paula Orange said. "Not book smart but intuitive. She could read people."

Sheila was born Sheila Kaye Bailey in Fort Payne, Alabama in 1958.

She was the youngest of six children. Her first marriage with a man named Ronnie Jennings would last less than two months. Jennings would find out that Sheila had been locking his child from a previous marriage in a closet to punish her. Jennings would divorce Sheila but she would find herself a new man in short order, tying the knot with John Baxter and moving to Chattanooga, Tennessee. Even though married, she would secretly fantasize about being swept away by a rich man. Sheila's mental illness would come to bear in her second marriage and that would end in divorce as well. Despondent, Sheila tried to kill herself and was sent to a psychiatric facility. She would be raped by an orderly inside the hospital.

Now single in Tennessee, the cash-strapped Sheila was forced to live in a local YMCA. She attended a church service and had a private talk with one of the preachers as she wanted "spiritual guidance." She would later claim that the reverend asked if she wanted to "sit in his lap." She then went to a psychiatrist who asked her if she had anal sex with any of her former husbands. The doctor then called Sheila at home and asked if "what she was wearing" and if she "was touching herself."

"If what we are to believe all of Sheila's stories," Orange said. "Then literally all of her interactions with men have ended with them as the pervert and her as the victim. Her sister would later testify that Sheila was molested by her father when she was young. Then her abusive marriages, the rape at the psych facility segues into a spiritual search where she meets a preacher who shows her the tent in his pants. Crazy."

CHAPTER TWO

Sheila turned to personal ads after her failures in marriage. She didn't like the normal courtship process of going to bars and meeting men there. She used the personal ads to cherry pick the men she wanted, men she could dominate.

"Whether on-line or off-line, Sheila behaved like a woman who was in complete control," Orange said. "She would develop a strange kind spf power over men. It was almost as if she knew which men would be vulnerable to her feminine wiles and which ones would fight back. But when it came to Dr. Bill LaBarre, it was more of a case of getting the money."

While in Tennessee, Dr. LaBarre decided to take out a personal ad. He would get a response from Sheila who immediately sought to separate herself from the other paramours of the rich doctor.

She sent the doctor nude Polaroids of herself.

The strategy worked.

"She showed no shame in flirting with the older man and soon had him in the palm of her hand," Orange said. "He'd buy her fancy clothes, necklaces, the whole nine yards."

Wilfred "Bill" LaBarre was a successful chiropractor but lonely. Overweight and bespectacled, he had little to offer aside from his wealth. He was in his sixties and recently widowed.

Dr. Labarre was considered a good man by all who knew him. He had been the "Chiropractor of the Year" in 1983 but that would be the same year his beloved Edwina would pass away from cancer. Eager to salve the loneliness, he married another woman named Leona but she abandoned the doctor after a few years. He had two children from his first marriage; Laura and Gregory.

Now alone and widowed, the doctor wanted to spend his golden years enjoying his wealth.

And a young woman.

He would look at the nude Polaroids of the curvaceous Southern Belle, becoming obsessed.

"Here was a lonely, older man who all of a sudden had a 27-year old woman sending him nude photos. He thought he hit the jackpot."

Dr. LaBarre soon invited Sheila to come live with him at his farm in Epping, New Hampshire. The farm was a spacious one, a 115-acre horse ranch that according to LaBarre, "needed a female hand."

Sheila would become enamored by life on the farm, at least at first. She "never heard a June bug before" and the isolated country home gave her a peace that she never experienced.

Neighbors were not shocked that Dr. LaBarre took in such a younger woman as his girlfriend. He reportedly had other girlfriends after his wife died. "Sheila ran all the other girls off," one neighbor said.

But Sheila would prove to be a high-maintenance girlfriend. She would drain Dr. LaBarre's finances, making him buy her gifts and prizes which included a brand-new Silver Mercedes.

She also began to interject herself into LaBarre's estate and business dealings.

The farm that LaBarre owned was called the Old Harvey Farm. It was named after the original owners of the property who still lived in the area. But Sheila forced the doctor to change the name, she wanted it called something that reflected her personality.

The Silver Leopard Farm.

Sheila then had a sign made up and had it placed at the entrance.

She was marking her territory.

CHAPTER THREE

Despite the constant gifts and financial prizes, Sylvia proved to be an ungrateful sugar baby. The relationship would turn tempestuous after a few months. Sheila would claim that Dr. LaBarre often referred to himself as an "old fart" and looked the other way when Sheila began to have different men over for sex.

"He just worried about me when I would date far from home. But he was getting old and his heart would stop beating sometimes."

But the couple fought and police were routinely called to the residence to mediate their domestic disputes.

"You would sometimes hear gunshots," Bruce Allen, a LaBarre neighbor said. "You would hear her screaming, 'I'm going to kill you, you mother fucker!'"

Sheila once pulled a gun on the doctor and forced him out of the home. The chiropractor hid behind a boulder as his girlfriend shot at him.

LaBarre's daughter also recalled that she heard Sheila screaming threats at her father. "I'm gonna kill the horses and I'm going to kill you too."

Laura would later remark at how much her father changed after Sheila came into his life. He went from a normal, well-liked member of the community to a meek, submissive man.

"Sheila was all about being an opportunist," Orange said. "She had the ability to read a man, analyzing his weaknesses, size him up and then push the buttons. With LaBarre, she had a lonely man in front of her. He would tolerate anything in order not to lose her at first and then he simply became fearful of his life. These men in this small New England town did not have the wherewithal to deal with a violent sociopath like Sheila."

Sheila didn't stop with the renaming of Old Harvey Home. She soon took over the accounting duties at LaBarre's chiropractic business. She began organizing the practice into a well-oiled machine. She would track down patients who owed the doctor money and file numerous small claims in the Hampton District Court.

Concerned friends would advise him to dump Sheila before it was too late but it became apparent that the doctor either didn't know how or was afraid to. Dr. LaBarre informed neighbor Bruce Allen that he "had to get rid of her" and that he wanted to "send her back to Alabama. Hopefully, she'll stay there."

Her power over Dr. LaBarre increased to the point where he had given her power of attorney. She began rewriting his will, becoming the executor of his estate. The will stated that he was leaving everything to "a very special lady known as Sheila Kaye Jennings LaBarre."

"The will was very carefully redacted from the original," Orange said. "She kept a lot of the parts of the original and used her own typewriter to amend the little detail of where all the assets will go to. She was very astute and covered her tracks very well for someone who was supposedly schizophrenic."

The two would live together (Sheila would move out briefly but claim to be his common-law wife) from 1987 until LaBarre's death in 2000 at the age of 74. The coroner logged his cause of death as heart disease. There were suspicions among those close to the doctor that believe Sheila poisoned him to hasten the process.

"He was pretty old," Orange said. "And according to the autopsy, the heart disease was significant. So Sheila didn't have anything to do with his death despite the suspicions. The killings would come later."

Sheila would inherit the farm, LaBarre's Chiropractor office, two apartments and a rental home.

This was all valued at over two million dollars in assets.

Strangely, Sheila would marry a Jamaican national named Wayne Ennis in August of 1995 while living with Dr. LaBarre. Ennis drove a tour bus around Jamaica and Sheila made sure that when she toured the islands with Dr. LaBarre that they would cross paths with her Jamaican lover. She arranged for Ennis to obtain a visa and took him back to the farm with her. She would later claim that she and the doctor had stopped having sex and that she "had needs" which apparently Ennis took care of. She would later concede to pleasing the doctor sexually, "I'd use my hand," she said afterward.

Ennis would live in the farmhouse for almost a year. He had his own numerous encounters with Sheila which were violent and bizarre. One night, she ordered him to get in the car. The two then drove around the quiet town, Sheila's voice taking on a conspiratorial tone.

"I wish one of those damn horses would just kick him (Dr. LaBarre) in the head," Sheila said. "Kick him in the head and kill his old ass. I've thought about strangling him myself. But now I have a better idea. I want you to kill him."

Ennis was too frightened to say no to Sheila. The two would eventually divorce and the court records reveal that Sheila took out a restraining order against him.

Ennis disputed the allegations and stated that Sheila was the abuser.

He would later recall being punched, pushed, and shot at by Sheila.

"She told me that she was going to send me back to Jamaica in a box," Ennis said.

Dr. LaBarre told Ennis that Sheila was crazy and believed that she would eventually kill him. He gave the Jamaican money and sent him to the bus station, requesting that he leave town for his own safety.

After the relationship with Ennis ended, Sheila began dating James Brackett.

She and James would remain together for six years despite the fact that Sheila would attack Brackett with a pair of scissors, a machete, and an ax. When all of that failed she tried to shoot him.

The two would break up after which Brackett would get himself a vanity license plate that read "I'm Alive."

Brackett recalled moments where Sheila would act sweet and nice only to go into a violent rage moments later. He said that the greatest example was a time when he was taking a long bath with Sheila only to have her get out of the tub and smash him in the face with a two-foot grill brush.

Two of his teeth would be knocked out from the impact.

Sheila would attack Brackett for a variety of transgressions that would not be guilty of. Hurting her rabbits, damaging her property or having affairs with other women.

Brackett finally had enough, escaping from the farm on one rainy night and hitchhiking back into town.

"I'm lucky to be alive," he would later state.

CHAPTER FOUR

Sheila inherited the farm after LaBarre's death. The doctor's children tried to contest the will but were told that the odds of winning the case were 50/50 at best. They would also have to front over $50,000 to pay for the court costs.

Sheila soon turned the farm into her own private fiefdom. She would hire young men to help her around the place then pay them with her sexual favors or sometimes just beat the shit out of them.

"There would neighbors that would claim to see young men leave her house," Orange said. "They would look beaten up; black eyes, bloody lips, facial contusions. God knows what else."

Her neighbors began to suspect something fishy was going on but had no real evidence to call the police with.

"The first time I met Sheila LaBarre was at the Harvey Farm Stand," said Bonnie Meroth, one of Sheila's neighbors. "It was during the summertime when the produce was ready. I had no basic interaction with her except that of someone standing next to another person as a consumer. And she suddenly turned around and said 'I'll kill you if you come down to my farm' or words to that effect."

Bonnie would later claim that Sheila would try to scare her while driving down the road, nearly running her over while she was on her morning walk.

When she wasn't intimidating neighbors and townsfolk, Sheila would use the farm as the playground for her own private fetishes.

She liked to control and bully men. Stroking one of her pet rabbits, she would punish and insult the men unlucky enough to work at her farm.

"Are you kidding me?" Sheila yelled at the young man who dropped the wheelbarrow. "This should have been done yesterday."

He was young and naive, needing money. If it meant taking lip from Sheila, so be it. He needed work and she seemed nice when she hired him.

"Hurry up!" Sheila said, kicking the man in his buttocks. "Move, move. Are you kidding me? I've never seen a lazier man in my life."

Fatigued after working sixteen hours for seven days straight, the young man keeled over in exhaustion, dropping the wheelbarrow.

"Bitch made, perverted ass pedophile!" Sheila said. "Is this what I am paying you for? I am paying you to work. Now get off your bitch ass. Now!"

It became apparent that Sheila had a gift. A gift of controlling a certain type of man. Verbally abusive and overbearing, she encountered very little resistance.

She kicked the young man again. "Your name is 'bitch', you hear me?"

His real name was Michael Deloge.

CHAPTER FIVE

Deloge had problems as a teen. He got caught up in drugs and found himself on the streets, living out of homeless shelters. In 2004, he would meet Sheila LaBarre.

Deloge became smitten with the woman whom he saw as the life of the party. She would drink beer and play country songs on a guitar. According to Deloge's stepfather, Gordon Boston, the duo would indulge in drugs and study "sadistic material".

Deloge would join Sheila at her farm and soon become her personal whipping boy. Sheila would slap him around like a rag doll. One of the fellow ranch hands, Philip Sullos, recalled witnessing Sheila beating on Deloge with a hardwood stick until he bled. Deloge cowered and took the beating. She would then throw Deloge into a windowless shack and slam the door shut.

Deloge would cower meekly in the corner until Sheila came and got him, making no attempt to escape.

He would be declared missing in 2004 and no one would ever see him again.

In February of 2006, Sheila began looking for a new farmhand. She had her own criteria. He had to be young but pliable to her controlling methods.

She would find the perfect foil in Kenny Countie.

"Kenny was a lovely boy," Carolynn Lodge, Kenny's mother said. "He couldn't do enough for you. Everyone was his friend. I was so proud of him. He never had a horrible word for anybody and that was the problem. He trusted everybody."

Kenny's trust would lead him into Sheila LaBarre's trap.

Kenny would answer one of Sheila's personal ads. The young man was still naive and according to some reports had a "low IQ". The two met through a telephone personal ad service with Sheila calling up the young man and charming him in a way that no woman ever did.

"He (Kenny) told my son Brian that he met a 47-year old woman in New Hampshire," Lodge said. "She owned a farm. She owned a beautiful car. And she was rich. And he was serious about her."

"Kenny fit Sheila's psychological criteria," Orange said. "She targeted men whom she could overpower not only physically but also mentally. She was older than Kenny and light years more cunning. She knows exactly what to say and do to push his buttons. She takes the lead, telling him that he is going to be 'in for the time of his life' and that she 'can't wait to see him.' To a young man with limited experience and intelligence like Kenny, this is music to his ears."

Sheila would arrive at Kenny's home in the silver Mercedes. The silver leopard, the cougar, picking up her prey and taking him back to her lair.

Kenny's family would never see him again.

Sheila would use the same methods on Kenny as she did on the men in the past. She seduced the young man first then isolated him in her farmhouse. Then she berated him verbally before beating the shit out of him with face slaps, punches, and a wooden stick.

The beatings would come to a head during a weekend in February of 2000. Sheila beat Kenny's face into a pulp, took the wooden cane to his legs and may have poisoned him.

Then she decided to take him shopping at Walmart.

Placing him in a wheelchair, she rolled him around the outlet as she stocked up on garden supplies. She dumped two containers of diesel fuel into the prone Kenny's lap.

Little did he know that she would later use the gas to incinerate his body.

Customers gawked at the odd couple, concerned about the contusions on Kenny's face.

"Fuck you looking at?" Sheila would scream as she sped down through the aisle.

Employees of the store soon became concerned, calling the police.

The cops would arrive, confronting the couple in the store. They inquired about Kenny's condition but he didn't respond. Instead, Sheila took the lead, telling Kenny that he "didn't have to talk to these assholes."

The police didn't follow through. Kenny remained silent as Sheila rolled him through the store and out the door. No crime had been witnessed and they let the couple go.

Kenny's mother would later sue the police for negligence but it was tossed out of court in 2010.

A few nights after the Walmart incident, Sheila would make a frantic phone call to the police.

"I got a pervert in my house!" she screamed into the phone. "He's a pedophile! A pedophile!"

In a bizarre sequence of events, Sheila began to play a recording for the detective on the other end. She had routinely audio recorded everything she did, trying to incriminate the young men she worked with into admitting they were pedophiles. On this occasion, she played back a recording of her and Kenny.

"On the tape was my son, vomiting," Lodge said. "He kept saying 'he's faking, he's faking.'"

Sheila would ask Kenny if he was a pedophile on the tape. Kenny would answer 'yes'.

"Now he's a pedophile," Kenny's mother said. "Now he's raping children. Raping his brother. He's vomiting."

The police would write off the call as the rantings of a schizophrenic. They did not immediately respond to the residence.

Sheila would then kill Kenny Countie.

"She had to justify the killing of the young men in her own mind," Orange said. "For some bizarre reason, she would brainwash herself into thinking that her victims were pedophiles. She would repeat the question like a mantra, 'Are you a pedophile? Are you a pedophile?' Working herself up into an angry and violent state of mind before she killed the man."

Sheila's sister, Lynn Noojin, believed that Sheila was sexually abused by her father. Because of this, she became obsessed with child molestation. She would accuse the young men that worked for her of various sexual deviations, including pedophilia, incest, and bestiality.

CHAPTER SIX

After the bizarre call to police, authorities would not arrive at the farmhouse until the next morning. The police would enter the grounds, seeing both the burning mattress and barrel with Kenny's remains. They would not identify the burning bones as belonging to Kenny until much later.

Sheila had murdered Kenny the night before. She attacked Kenny ferociously with a kitchen knife, pushing the already weakened young man to the floor and stabbing away.

Blood sprayed and splattered everywhere.

Sheila then dragged Kenny's body out to her yard where she doused his body with the diesel fuel they had purchased at Walmart.

Lighting a match, she set the dead man on fire. She then took her pet rabbit in her lap, pulled up a chair and watched Kenny Countie burn.

"He was dismembered," Kenny's mother said, fighting tears. "And he was put in a pit and burned. But my son, he just wanted to be loved. I can't imagine what he must have been thinking. Because he was all alone."

Police would look throughout the house and find blood splatter on the walls and floor. A forensic team arrived and matched the blood with Kenny's DNA sample from his Army days. They would find the wallet of Michael Deloge but not his body.

Hundreds of police would spend seventeen days searching the 115-acre property. They found numerous burn pits and blood remains that were so old they had layers of dust on them. They would find clothing that belonged to Deloge and some toes that remain unidentified (it is rumored that the toes may belong to a mysterious Irish man who Sheila claims was stalking her.)

Going on the run from the cops, Sheila hitchhiked along Interstate 293. She was then picked up by Stephen Martello.

"Thanks so much for stopping," Sheila said.

"No problem," Martello said, looking the buxom Southern Belle up and down. His heart began to race.

Will he get lucky?

"My car broke down about two miles back. I got into a fight with my boyfriend and I'm trying to get to Dorchester."

"I'm headed that way," Martello said.

Sheila clutched her purse as if it were a security blanket and she kept looking back at the rear window.

"You all right?" he asked.

"Yeah," Sheila said "Just a little rattled. You know, it has been a tough day."

Martello took Sheila to the drug store when she said she needed to stop off and "buy some things". He tailed Sheila around the store until she bought a douche. Noting her erratic behavior, Martello disappeared out of Sheila's earshot to call the police on his cell phone.

"Hi," Martello said. "Just curious if you folks are looking for someone who just robbed a bank or an escaped mental patient. I just met a woman who is acting kind of strange."

When the authorities informed him that they were not actively investigating someone with that kind of background, Martello took Sheila to a hotel room.

The two would engage in wild and loud sex.

"You just had sex with an angel," Sheila proclaimed after they were done.

"Is that right?"

"You're not like the other men," Sheila said. "My boyfriend, Jesus, I just caught him with a huge stack of child porn. He is a pedophile. So are all those damn cops. Pedophiles, all of them. I think all sex offenders must die."

Martello said nothing. Instead, he put his pants and shoes on as fast as he could as Sheila continued to go on another bizarre rant.

"Vengeance is mine saith the Lord," Sheila said, laying on the bed in post-coital repose. "I was sent back to earth as an angel. I know how to speak to God in Hebrew. Do it every night."

Martello excused himself and high-tailed it out of the hotel room. He arrived home and saw the television broadcast about Sheila. He didn't call the police, worried that he would be an accessory to her crimes. Instead, Martello drove to the station and practically sprinted to the front desk.

"I think I just met Sheila LaBarre."

"To the end, Sheila had control over just about every man put in front of her," Orange said. "Here was a guy who picks her up at the side of the road. He thinks she is crazy enough to where he calls the cops to find out if there are any missing mental patients. He knows that she has a screw loose but he has sex with her anyway. It may be a poor reflection on men for sure but his response is typical. The men that Sheila encountered, from Dr. LaBarre all the way to Stephen Martello, all had the same false narratives going on in their head. They did not see a beautiful woman as something evil. It just didn't fit their narrative. So when Sheila begins her abuse, they just can't believe it. They refuse to hit a 'woman' back. She gets them 'pussy whipped' then beats the shit out of them. Rinse and repeat."

Sheila LaBarre would later be arrested for the murders of Michael Deloge and Kenneth Countje. She would plead no guilty on the grounds of insanity.

"This is a sick, sick woman," her attorney would argue. "Deeply disturbed."

Court-appointed psychiatrists would agree, testifying that Sheila was delusional as well as schizophrenic.

The jury would visit both LaBarre's farm and the Walmart where she frequented first hand. Sheila would join them as well although she was forced to wear a stun belt.

The jury did not buy her insanity defense and found her guilty.

"The fact that she has to remain for the rest of her life behind bars," Kenny's mother said. "She got what she asked for. She'll never see the light of day. Horrible thing is that my son, he's not here with me. He was only twenty-four."

Sheila LaBarre is now serving life in without possibility of parole.

KILLER OR CHRISTIAN?

The True Story of Karla Faye Tucker

94

BECCA BENTON

"My change doesn't bring back any of those lives. But society shouldn't want me to stay in a 'killer' frame of mind. That's okay if they say change doesn't matter as far as 'no, she shouldn't get off on death row' or 'yes, she should be executed.' But surely they wouldn't want me to stay in a killer frame of mind. You think? I hope not." - Karla Faye Tucker

"She always said someday she would be famous." - Steven Griffith, Karla's ex-husband.

There are numerous competing stories regarding the life and persona of Karla Faye Tucker. There is one camp that considers her to be one of the vilest killers in modern Texas history. Then there is another camp who believes that she underwent a religious conversion in prison and that her life should have been spared.

Karla Faye Tucker murdered two people in 1983. She would convert to Christianity upon entering prison and a movie was produced that chronicled her life and reformation. Fifteen years after she committed her crime she would be put to death by lethal injection.

Did she really change? Does it even matter?

This is the story of Karla Faye Tucker, one that resonates almost twenty years after her execution.

GOING NOWHERE FAST

"Karla was a problem child," forensic psychologist Paula Orange said. "No one expressed shock at her behavior when she was arrested for murder. It was almost as if they expected her to do something really bad. Karla was on the fast train to hell at an early age."

Karla was the youngest of three sisters, born and raised in Houston, Texas.

The family did have some good times. Sister Kari Ann was one year older than Karla while Kathi Lynn was two. The family had a German Shepherd and took summer vacations in Caney Creek in Texas where her father Larry owned a cottage.

"I was an itty-bitty girl," Karla recalled during a 700 Club interview. "We were family, and we used to go to the bay house and do neat things with the boat and dog and water skiing and fishing and stuff, but it didn't last very long."

Her father worked as a longshoreman while her mother was a secretary. Her mother was quite pretty and her father had a rugged handsomeness. In their photos together, they look to be a loving and good looking couple with the world as their oyster. But their relationship was tumultuous and the couple would begin a long cycle of breaking up then getting back together again. They would finally divorce when Karla was ten. It was during the divorce testimonies that Karla would find out that she had been the product of an extra-marital affair. This explained to Karla why she always felt inferior to her older sisters who were blonde-haired and blue-eyed. Karla was an odd duck with a screechy voice and a large birthmark on her arm.

"I don't know why my parents divorced; I was too young to know," Karla said. "My dad got custody of us girls, and we all wanted to go with Mother…My father couldn't control us real good. He tried to discipline us, but we were just too much, just too much."

Karla was almost always the smallest girl in her class. Early photos showed her to be a tomboyish looking girl with a bright and vivacious smile. But Karla had begun using drugs in elementary school and she never stopped. The highs and lows of her drug addiction led to her already short fuse growing even smaller.

"Karla was a very violent person," homicide detective J.C. Mosier said. "She would fight with you in a minute. A man or a woman. She got into many barroom fights. She was a tough little gal but she never had anywhere to go but prison. She was destined for prison."

"Some people end up being cheerleaders," Karla said. "And end up in that circle. I ended up on the opposite end of the totem pole. I wasn't born a bad person. And I don't always have to be a bad person."

"She had two strikes against her but they were very big," Orange said. "She grew up in direct vicinity to a drug epicenter in Houston. The neighborhood she was in was rife with drug use and it was the thing to do for all of the kids to just fit in. Karla herself would talk often about peer pressure but was careful to not lay responsibility for her behavior on anyone but herself. Her second strike was her own mother who modeled the worst behavior imaginable for all three of her daughters."

A lot of blame has focused on Karla's mother who led her on the path to destruction.

"Her mother was a drug addict and a prostitute," Mosier said. "But she always had a normal, square day job as a secretary."

Karla's mother brought her daughters up with no rules or lines that you couldn't cross. Karla could do whatever she wanted and to hell with anyone who got in her way. For example, Karla didn't learn how to roll up a joint from her ne'er-do-well friends at school or around the neighborhood.

She learned from her own mother.

"She had gotten caught with rolling up a joint in the house," Orange said. "Her mother caught her and instead of chastising her for having drugs in the house she criticized her for not knowing how to properly roll a joint. But being the good mother that she was, she immediately gave Karla instructions on 'how to roll up a doobie.'"

DO AS I SAY EVEN IF IT KILLS YOU

Karla's mother had introduced both her and her sisters to drugs. Karla would follow the lead of all three and hang out with a biker gang in the neighborhood who called themselves the "Banditos." Karla would go to a lot of their parties and would lose her virginity to one of the bikers when she was only twelve years old. The biker had talked her into joining him in a lover's lane spot where they did drugs and he had sex with the underage girl. Karla, however, enjoyed the experience as it made her believe that "sex on high was the ultimate trip."

She had a devil-may-care attitude toward life. Her academic studies were non-existent as she was a constant discipline problem at school.

"Her teachers had given up on her," writer Linda Strom said. "Her mom was living her own life. A party life. Encouraging Karla to go with her into that lifestyle. Karla herself would start smoking marijuana when she was eight. So by the time she was twelve she was shooting heroin."

Karla's father could not fare better with the girls although he tried harder than his ex-wife. Problem was, he would never be home to enforce any discipline. Larry Tucker would work two 16-hour shifts and be absent from the home with the girls got back from school.

"This was a Lord of the Flies scenario if there ever was one," Orange said. "You have three pre-teen girls with no supervision. Absolutely none. Their mother wasn't an adult herself so how the hell could she raise three girls?"

"Karla was doomed from the beginning. Her mother got her into prostitution and coached her in sexual techniques. So when we are discussing her childhood we have to say that it was very, very brief. There was no extended adolescence here. Her mother robbed her of her innocence probably from the day she was born. Karla never had a chance."

At the age of fourteen, Karla began working as a prostitute...at her mother's lead.

"Her mother was her idol," Strom said.

"(My mother) took me to a place where there was all men and wanted to school me in the art of being a call girl," Karla recalled. "I wanted to please my mother so much. I wanted her to be proud of me. So, instead of saying no, I just tried to do what she asked...The thing is, I knew deep down inside that what I was doing was wrong."

Karla's mother was a rock groupie in addition to being a prostitute. In addition to hanging out with the biker gangs, the two would travel with the Eagles, The Marshall Tucker Band, and the Allman Brothers.

AN ATTEMPT AT DOMESTICITY

At the age of sixteen, Karla married a mechanic by the name of Stephen Griffin.

The couple started off well enough. Stephen fell in love with Karla's tomboy ways and her willingness to stand up for both herself and him.

"We fist-fought a lot," Stephen recalled. "I've never had men hit me as hard as she did. Whenever we went into a bar, I didn't have to worry because she had my back covered."

But Stephen soon realized that he had married damaged goods. When they got high, drunk or even had sex it was all well-plowed soil for Karla. She was a wild horse that needed to be set free.

It would not take long for Karla to decide that married life and the prospect of having children was not in the cards for her. She left Stephen and returned to her old ways of hanging out with biker gangs.

"Karla appeared to have tried that straight road for awhile," Orange said. "She had the type of personality that would try just about anything once. Still, Stephen Griffin is lucky he came out of that relationship alive. It was the typical teenage puppy love we are going to be forever type of thing at first. Then he found out that Karla is a whole different kind of sick puppy."

Karla spent her remaining teen years on into her twenties partying it up in the low-rent housing projects of Houston. She did it all and loved it. Booze. Cocaine. Heroin. And lots of sex.

She would eventually meet an older man in Danny Garrett and the two hit it off immediately. Danny didn't judge her for being a prostitute and supplied her with drugs.

"Karla just could not stay away from the whole biker drug scene," Orange said. "It was all she knew. Some kids have parents who are doctors and nurses and they do likewise. Karla was at the opposite end of the spectrum. Her mother was a whore who serviced rock musicians and biker scum. Karla had resigned herself to the same life."

LIGHTING THE FUSE

Karla had become friends with Shawn Dean, one of the "biker mommas" that used to hang out at the same parties. Shawn was deferential and timid while Karla was fiery and aggressive. The two were fire and ice.

Shawn had a boyfriend named Jerry whom Karla took an instant dislike to. She didn't like men with big egos and particularly did not like men who beat on their women, especially if that woman was her best friend.

Jerry was an obnoxious loud mouth. The guy had rolled his motorcycle inside Karla's house one day and dripped oil over the carpet. Karla got pissed, complaining about the exhaust fumes stinking up the house. Karla and Jerry had words and she kicked both he and Shawn out of her home. The two would have altercations a few times after that with one violent episode.

"One time he was sitting in his car outside," Karla recalled. "And I punched him in the eye for just being there."

Jerry Dean was typical Texas biker trash. He had long hair, squinted eyes and the facial expression of someone who was perpetually high.

His beatings on Shawn began to increase an intensity, open palmed slaps soon turned into closed fist punches.

The abuse was both physical and verbal. Karla decided to interject herself on Shawn's behalf on many occasions which led to his increasing dislike of her. There was an instance where someone had found a picture of Karla posing with her mother. Jerry took hold of the picture and slammed a butcher knife through the photo, enraging Karla.

"Jerry and Karla had a bad relationship," prosecuting attorney Joe Magliolo said. "Allegedly he had cut up some pictures of Karla and her mom which really upset Karla to the point where she had actually hit him, broke his glasses and cut his eye."

The feud between Jerry and Karla would come to a head on June 13th, 1983.

A three-day party had taken place in Karla's home where she had lived with Danny aka "The Pill Doctor." The celebration was for Karla's older sister Kari Ann. Karla's sister wanted an orgy of sex and drugs. Karla and Danny provided that and more.

"Who wants dessert?" Danny called out as he entered the living room with a tray of uppers and downers; dilaudids, valium, mandrex, and placydils.

"Woot! Woot!" Karla's sister Kari did cartwheels in the living room.

The party goers wasted no time in getting high while others indulged in both the drugs and sex.

'I had been doing a considerable amount of coke and bathtub speed," Karla recalled. "I didn't usually do speed much; heroin and downers was my preference because I am a very hyper person and doing speed always 'skitzed' me out made me go crazy...(That night) we were cooking speed, and we started shooting it because it was there, and I loved the needle in my arm. I was what one would call a needle freak."

Karla's friend Shawn arrived at the party with a bloodied nose and a busted lip. She had left Jerry a week earlier but he caught up with her again, getting in another beating which she would not report. Karla saw what her arch enemy did to her best friend and went ballistic.

"I saw what he had done to (Shawn), and I was really mad (because) I was really protective of her," Karla Faye said. "I thought, 'Yeah, I'll get even with him!' My idea of getting even with him meant confronting him, standing toe to toe, fist to fist."

Initially, Karla did not plan to kill Jerry. She just wanted to give him the same treatment he had given poor Shawn.

Karla popped pill after pill, the drugs fueling her need for revenge. While other party goers danced and frolicked with hazy brains, Karla stewed. She ordered Shawn, Danny and a friend named Jimmy Leibrant to the kitchen in order to discuss how they were going to get back at Jerry.

"I want to beat the living shit out of him," Karla slammed her palm on the kitchen counter.

"Damn, take it easy girl," Danny said.

"Take it easy nothing," Karla grabbed Shawn's face and turned it to Danny. "Does that look like taking it easy?"

"Fine," Danny shrugged his shoulders before swallowing a handful of uppers. "Let's go whip his ass."

"You guys-" Shawn started but stopped when Karla's sister Kari and her boyfriend Ron entered the kitchen. The idle threats soon turned into jokes with each person describing in exaggerated terms just how bad they would kick Jerry's ass.

"These were very immature young people in a drug haze," Orange said. "There was not one rational thinking person in the entire group. They had spent their entire lives chasing the next high and really had no idea of the consequences of their actions simply because there never were any. The answer to Shawn's problem was never to leave and never come back. The answer is to kick Jerry Dean's ass. And they wound up killing him."

Danny left the party that evening for his bartender job. Karla drove him to work and would come back at two o'clock in the morning to pick him up when his shift ended.

After dropping her boyfriend off, Karla returned to her home with most of the party goers now gone. Shawn remained and told Karla her tale of woe over a bottle of tequila. Her vivid descriptions of his abuse only enraging Karla even more.

"Karla really didn't like men very much," Orange said. "She inherited this hatred from her mother. When she set her sights on getting revenge on Jerry Dean he became the sum total of every man that ever done her wrong in life. Karla didn't just have baggage when it came to men. She had a whole freight load of it. And she was going to take it all out on Jerry Dean."

THE ROBBERY

The home invasion started out as a simple burglary. Karla wanted to give Jerry a scare while her boyfriend Danny looked to steal the biker's motorcycle. They both saw that as the ultimate sign of disrespect. Stealing a biker's Harley Davidson.

Karla and Danny were joined by James Leibrant as they drove up to Jerry Dean's apartment at three o'clock in the morning on Monday, June 13th, 1983. Leibrant stayed outside as he went looking for Dean's car. Karla and Denny entered the apartment without breaking in. Karla had the keys to the door, finding them after Shawn said that they were "lost."

The couple entered the bedroom and Karla sat on Dean. Jerry then grabbed onto Karla and the two struggled. Danny pulled them apart, smashing Danny over the head numerous times with a hammer that he found on the floor. He struck Jerry with such force that his head separated from his neck and his breathing passages began to fill with fluid. Danny then ransacked the house, finding the motorcycle parts that he wanted and taking them to his truck.

Meanwhile, Karla grew irritated at the "gurgling sound" coming from Dean and wanted to "stop him from making that noise."

Karla found a pick ax next to Dean's bed, something he was using perhaps as a weapon for home defense.

"Karla started swinging the ax on Jerry," Mosier said. "I think it was an accumulation of booze and drugs and her intense hate for Jerry. Jerry was struck around thirty-five times, as I remember."

What Karla didn't know was that Deborah Thornton was sleeping next to Jerry.

She had tried to remain as quiet as possible but an errant strike of the ax had struck her in the shoulder.

Karla pulled the covers back to reveal Deborah. She hesitated for a moment then her criminal mind kicked in.

Deborah was a witness, she had to be killed.

Karla attacked, grazing Deborah in the shoulder with the ax. Deborah fought back and the two grappled before Danny came into the room and separated the two.

Deborah was in such pain that she begged the duo to just kill her.

"'Just please kill me,'" Orange said. "She didn't plead for her life. She wanted them to get it over with. She was in the wrong place at the wrong time. They were both married to other people. They had just met in a bar and Jerry had taken her home."

Karla was only too happy to oblige as she slammed away with the pick-axe. Blood splattered the air. Later Karla would brag that she had experienced an orgasm with every blow she hit Deborah with.

Danny would egg Karla on. He covered Deborah with a blanket and encouraged Karla to drive the pick-axe into her body.

"Come on!" he screamed. "Pretend it is a piñata."

The last blow struck Deborah in the chest, impaling her.

With that, the couple would grab up as many motorcycle parts as they could and leave the apartment.

"It was a horrible scene of violence," Mosier said. "It left a lot of us, even those who had thought we had seen it all, just amazed at the brutality of the crime."

Karla and Danny were not out to commit the perfect crime and get away with it. Instead, Karla went around bragging about the murder, telling anyone who would listen how she pick-axed the couple to death. She felt that it would add to her reputation as the toughest, craziest bitch in Houston.

"I not only didn't walk around with any guilt," Karla recalled. I was proud of thinking I had finally measured up to the big boys. I didn't care about anybody...I didn't place any value on myself or anybody else."

A co-worker of Dean discovered the bodies the next morning as he was waiting for him to come pick him up. The police were called and it didn't take long for them to establish who some of Dean's known associates were. They would use the testimony of Jimmy Leibrant as state's evidence, allowing the man to walk away as they prosecuted Karla and Danny.

OPEN AND SHUT CASE

The couple would go to the home of Danny's brother after the murder. Doug Garrett knew that the two had done something horrific and decided to secretly record their confession.

"Was both of them people asleep when you all went in there?" the police chief asked.

"Mmm hmmm," Danny said.

"Did you all take that ax over?"

"No," Doug said.

"It was already there?"

"Yeah," Karla said.

This audio recording along with the taped interrogation of the police chief would be enough for the prosecution to ask the courts for the death penalty.

"Did you enjoy the killings?" the police chief asked during Karla's interrogation.

"Hell yes!" she squealed.

The jury would be visibly sickened by Karla's lack of remorse on the audio.

"The tapes were her undoing," Orange said. "The jury was chilled to the bone. Had she shown some remorse, shed a crocodile tear or two then maybe she would have gotten a life sentence in lieu of the death penalty."

CONVERSION OR CON?

It was when she was imprisoned, however, that Karla claimed to have undergone a startling transformation.

She had gotten a hold of a Bible and began reading the book for the first time. Tears streamed down her face as she read page after page.

"As she read the Bible," Strom said. "Something hit her and for the first time realized what she had done. It's a genuine radical story of someone who is in darkness and walks into light."

"I think this was a real conversion," Mosier said. "I really think she became a Christian. A good person. It was a metamorphosis from what she was to what she became. It was really amazing and really true, in my mind, it really happened. She wasn't a phony. I don't think there was a phony bone in her body when she died."

Karla and Danny would be tried separately for the murders but her boyfriend would die of liver disease in 1993.

Karla would enter a plea of not guilty and proclaim to be a born-again Christian after her indictment. She would marry her prison minister, Reverend Dana Lane Brown, in 1995. The two would hold their wedding ceremony on prison grounds.

"The Lord put it in my heart," Brown said. "If you'll walk through the circumstances I'll deliver Karla into your arms. I knew that the Lord had spoke to my heart and we believe it and we're standing on it."

"Everybody loved her," Strom said. "I met officers who said 'my life was never the same after I met her., after I had that encounter with her.' I have to say that too."

Karla would appeal for a retrial numerous times between 1984 and 1992. She stated that she was under the influence of drugs at the time of the killings. Her story had drawn the attention of Pope John Paul II, televangelist Pat Robertson and Ronald Carlson who was the brother of Deborah Thornton.

All of them lobbied for Karla to be removed from death row.

"I'm pro death penalty," Robertson said. "But this is one case where I take an exception. This woman has clearly been transformed. To take her life now would not be a matter of justice. It would be vengeance."

Additionally, the warden of Huntsville prison testified on her behalf and stated that she had likely been reformed.

The husband of Deborah Thornton remained unconvinced of Karla's conversion. Despite his own wife cheating on him with Jerry Dean, he refused to believe in Karla's religious transformation.

"Gender politics and grandstanding played a key role in some of her apologists coming out," Orange said. "Religious leaders like the Pope and Pat Robertson refused to believe that women could be capable of such evil. A sweet-faced woman like Karla Faye Tucker was simply led astray like Mary Magdalene in their minds. All she needed was a little Jesus and she would turn out all right. You can contrast their position on Karla with their silence on Danny Garrett who was persona non grata."

Karla would write the following letter to the Texas Board of Paroles and Governor George W. Bush.

"I am in no way attempting to minimize the brutality of my crime. It obviously was very, very horrible and I do take full responsibility for what happened...I also know that justice and law demand my life for the two innocent lives I brutally murdered that night. If my execution is the only thing, the final act that can fulfill the demand for restitution for justice, then I accept that...I will pay the price for what I did in any way our law demands it...It was...three months after I had been locked up, when a ministry came to the jail and I went to the services, that night accepting Jesus into my heart. When I did this, the full and overwhelming weight and reality of what I had done hit me...I began crying that night for the first time in many years, and to this day, tears are part of my life...Fourteen years ago, I was part of the problem. Now I am part of the solution. I have purposed to do right for the last 14 years, not because I am in prison, but because my God demands this of me. I know right from wrong and I must do right...I don't really understand the guidelines for commutation of death sentences, but I can promise you this: If you commute my sentence to life, I will continue for the rest of my life in this earth to reach out to others to make a positive difference in their lives.

I see people in here in the prison where I am who are here for horrible crimes...I can reach out to these girls and try to help them change before they walk out of this place and hurt someone else."I am seeking you to commute my sentence and allow me to pay society back by helping others. I can't bring back the lives I took. But I can, if I am allowed, help save lives. That is the only real restitution I can give."

Governor Bush would not be impressed. Publicly, Bush described the pending execution as a "concrete in his chest, a decision that was weighing him down." But he would later be interviewed by conservative commentator Tucker Carlson who would describe Bush as having derision toward Karla and her supporters.

"I watched [Larry King's] interview with [Tucker], though," Bush said. "He asked her real difficult questions, like 'What would you say to Governor Bush?' "

"What was her answer?" Carlson asked.

"'Please,' Bush said going into a whiny impersonation of Karla. "'Don't kill me.' "

THE FINAL DAYS

"I'm not afraid of dying," Karla said before the execution. "I know that Jesus has already begun to prepare a place for me. I know if I have to go February 3rd that he is going to come and escort me personally. So I don't fear that. But I am certainly going to be concerned for those who are going to be left behind. For my family and friends. My husband."

"When she was getting ready to go to her execution," Strom said. "She said to me 'I'm praying that my execution will give those who can't forgive me the freedom to forgive so that they're free of this and don't have to spend their whole life dealing with what I've done."

For her last meal, Karla ordered a banana, a peach and a garden salad with ranch dressing. Karla would invite four people to watch her die; her sister Kari Weeks, husband Dana Brown, friend Jackie Oncken and Deborah Thornton's brother, Ronald Carlson.

"There was never any way out for Karla," Orange said. "From the moment, she was born it was as if she were doomed. Everything came too late for her. Whether her conversion was real or not, ultimately it is inconsequential to the lives of Jerry Dean and Deborah Thornton. They were truly the only ones who could forgive Karla."

On February 3rd, 1998, Karla was executed by lethal injection. As the lethal toxins went through her boy, Karla praised Jesus, licked her lips and looked to the ceiling above. She hummed for a few minutes then went silent. She was pronounced dead eight minutes after the injection.

"I love you, Karla!" her sister wailed.

"Just glowin'," Karla's husband, Rev. Dana Lane Brown said afterward. "The love of Jesus radiatin' through her and around her."

Karla would be buried at Forest Park Lawndale Cemetery in Houston.

"You have to think about others," Karla said in her final words with the 700 Club. "Every choice you make has an effect on somebody else's life. Every decision we make affects somebody else's life. And there are consequences whether they are positive or whether they are negative. We have to get back to the basics of what God says in the family and everything and we need to let our lives be governed by the morals of God by the integrity of God and until we do it is almost an 'I don't care' attitude. It's 'I don't care about others' I just only care about myself. Out there before I knew the Lord I always said I had to look out for number one. Which was me or nobody else would. But we know who number one is don't we? We know that number one is Jesus and number two is others and then us. And if we can really live our lives that way our world would be changed."

A MOTHER'S KILLER : THE TRUE STORY OF JENNIFER BAILEY

AMBER ULLMER

Imagine coming home after a hard day of work through the door to your quarter of a million dollar home. Then, hearing an eerie silence and nothing but darkness surrounding every inch of your four bedroom, two bathroom, roomy home. With a passing glance to the dining room and living room of your 3400-square-foot house, you head up the stairs with the goal of taking a warm bath and getting a fresh set of clothes for the night.

This is what Susan Bailey[1] did just before it happened. Two dozen stab wounds and two slashes to her throat cut that goal short with a spattering of blood on the wall and a coagulating pool of blood beneath her. She didn't expect to be killed that night. Neither did she expect it to be her own children who would do it to her.

Susan Marie Bailey grew up as a bubbly, funny, outgoing, and smart kid, according to her mother, Kate Morten. She had curly dark hair, was the second of four kids, and was extremely musically talented with the violin and clarinet. Susan was always a people-person. She wanted to do something at the intersection of business, fashion, and people. So, she went to college and earned a business and accounting degree at her local Minnesota college.

To get her fashion experience, Susan worked at Levi Strauss & Co. while in college. She still wanted to get out there more. Her life was a struggle in Minnesota with the snow stomping on her every attempt to be successful. She couldn't make it to work during the winter and work didn't stop just for the weather.

Susan had a difficult time commuting to work. She had to struggle through twenty miles of snow and ice every day. Months and months of brutal winter weather created snow drifts and blinding blizzards that became a routine. She requested to be moved to a closer store which they allowed her to do. Even though it became easier because she didn't have to drive that far in that bad of weather through the winter, it

---

1.   http://www.apple.com/

wasn't any easier in the Spring. An extra 28 inches of snow replaced pleasant Spring weather.

Then, one time when she had to close up shop after the other customers left and the cleaning had been done, she locked the front door and discovered an empty parking lot. Well, almost empty. Snow took over everything in sight, including her car.

Snow chilled her to the bone, darkness swallowed the town, and she was all alone. The snow was so high that she couldn't even open the doors to her car to get inside. So, she called her parents from a pay phone in a state of panic. She cried and in a fit of shivering from the cold she told her mother, "I'm never going to spend another winter in Minnesota." She did just that.

With that, Susan moved to California and built a successful clothing store. Then, she met her husband, Richard Bailey. Not so long after, she called up her mom with a startling message. "Mom, I'm married," Susan told her mother over a phone call in 1988, "Richard and I eloped."

Richard worked in the military and Susan was forced to follow him around while he was in the military. After he finished with the military, he took over caring for his kids and Susan worked. She worked extremely hard and took good care of her kids: Jennifer and David.

She worked two jobs to make sure that her kids could have anything and everything they ever wanted. Problems started when Jennifer was 18 and she wanted a 16-year-old guy named Paul Henson Jr. He was into Satanism, songs about death, and role-playing games. Of course, Jennifer's mother wasn't so thrilled about this and forbid her daughter to see the boy.

Similarly, 14-year-old Merrilee White wanted to be with Jennifer's boyfriend and she was willing to go to great lengths to do so. Her mother, Amy White, also didn't like Paul and told her not to see him. Meanwhile, little David Bailey just wanted to make his sister happy who oftentimes had to take care of him because the mom worked so much.

According to Donna Fielder, author of "Ladykiller," Paul Henson convinced the two that he had two personalities. Apparently, each girl was dating one of them.

Jennifer was scheduled to begin at an art college in a few days and the other three were supposed to start at Northwest Independent School District. Under the veil of appearing to be innocent teenagers, the four of them plotted for days. They planned on killing their parents so they could all be together, drive to Canada, and live happily ever after.

Paul, a 16-year-old with a double personality in which one was an executioner from the 18th century, had been dying to kill someone anyway. He wanted to know what it was like. So, Merrilee attempted to stab her sleeping mother who luckily talked her out of trying to stab her, Paul waited at home with a gun for his parents, and Jennifer Bailey waited at home for her hard-working mom to get home so she could kill her.

Jennifer Bailey was the only successful one out of the three. Susan Bailey was just coming home after leaving her second job in Fort Worth, Texas for the day. She returned home just in time. Jen, Paul, and David took turns stabbing Susan 26 times[2] in the throat after Paul's attempt to kill his parents didn't work.

On September 29, 2008, 11:31 AM, it was reported that 43-year-old Susan Bailey was found dead in her Roanoke home. The Tarrant County Medical Examiner's office claimed that she had multiple stab wounds to her neck. According to star-telegram.com[3], "Sgt. Chris Almonrode said officers had visited her home in the 200 block of Oxford Drive on Friday at the request of the woman's mother, who had grown concerned after not hearing from her daughter. He said

2.   http://donnakayefielder.blogspot.com/

3.   http://star-telegram.com/

officers could not get an answer at the door and found no evidence indicating that anything was wrong."

Kate Morten, Susan's mother, tried calling her daughter from her home in Minnesota. When no one answered, she called the Roanoke, Texas police. No one came to the door of their upscale home, so the Roanoke police burst into the door and found a murder scene.

They found the mother's body upstairs in the hallway sitting in a pool of her own blood. Foul play was immediately suspected as the cause of death. The Texas officers also found a bowl of poisoned pudding, a chunk of hair, and an electrical cord dangling right into a bathtub. Inside the bathtub sat three phones and a knife under a foot of water. Jennifer and David were going to kill their mother one way or another.

Meanwhile, a curious South Dakota cop [4]stopped Susan's car for violating town curfew and couldn't believe what he found. He pulled over Jennifer Bailey, 14-year-old David, and 16-year-old Paul in Susan's 2002 Saturn. He pulled them over at a closed gas station where they were trying to steal gas. They didn't have any money and their stories didn't make much sense. They had no real plan either.

He took them to the station and called the police in Roanoke, Texas. They knew about the kids and the woman that the car was registered to. The Tuesday before that week, Paul's father reported him a runaway and thought he was at Jennifer's house. The officers did not find him there. They did find his packed bags and a driver's license. Later on that day, they came back when Susan found a loaded magazine for a pistol, but the police couldn't find the gun.

Roanoke officers quickly put the pieces together after hearing that the three were together in Susan's car. At first, they didn't go straight in when the mother called worried about Susan because no one came to the door and the car was gone. When they found out about the kids,

---

4.	http://www.apple.com/

that's when they went in through the house through a window and found the dead mother.

The officer called Roanoke police and upon hearing what was happening, he held the three on suspicion of capital murder. They were all held at a juvenile detention facility in Sioux Falls, S.D.

Paul wasn't able to kill his parents, they decided to stay out late for a dinner and a movie, thankfully. Merrilee White, on the other hand, didn't get to kill her mother Amy White because luckily, she woke up before she could. The 15-year-old Fort Worth girl was detained on the 23rd of September after her mother reported that she woke up and found the girl standing over her with a knife. Merrilee was demanding that Amy give her her car keys. The girl later admitted to the police that she wanted to take her mother's car so that could take her friends to Canada.

When authorities went to investigate[5], they found notebooks, binders, and handwritten papers, computers, and discs that police described as, "pertaining to the preparation of murder." In the boyfriend's home, they found handwritten notes, papers, computers, discs, and "The Demonic Bible." As mentioned earlier, Paul loved to practice Satanism and was fond of all the things any parents wouldn't want their 17-year-old to be into. He was an avid fan of role-playing and fantasized frequently. Only, this wasn't done as a result of the fantasizing mind of a deranged 17-year-old; it was real.

On September 23rd, police called the Bailey home because they were looking for the boyfriend who was reported as a runaway. Susan and Jennifer fought over Paul. Police later came back later when Susan reported finding ammunition. The police searched the home and found a butcher knife in between the couch cushions and a knife under Jennifer's bed. Jennifer was showing signs of plans to kill early enough

---

5.   http://www.nbcdfw.com/news/local/
Affidavits_4_Teens_Planned_To_Kill_N_Texas_Mom.html

that it could have been prevented. However, her sweet mother had no clue that Jen would actually kill her.

Their school district, Northwest Independent School District, commented on this in an article published on September 29th in 2008 at approximately 11:31 AM. They said, "Our thoughts are with the families involved, and our school personnel continue to focus on the education and well being of our students. Should any child or staff member need to talk about the situation, school counselors are available." Too bad their counselors didn't notice earlier how unstable these four children were. Susan Bailey might still be alive.

Donna Fielder, as mentioned later, spoke to Kate, Susan's mom, who said that she still couldn't believe that her grandchildren would do such a terrible thing. Kate lived through the moment with baited breath from the phone call that drew silence from her deceased daughter to the announcement that her grandchildren killed their mother, her daughter.

What happened to the other three kids? [6]Jen stayed in the Denton County jail without bail and the boys stayed at the Denton Country Juvenile Facility. All three faced capital murder charges. They even tried to try Paul as an adult. In this case, he would serve out his Juvenile sentence and then finish up his sentence as an adult afterward. Under normal conditions[7], juvenile offenders were released from Texas Youth Commission when they would become adults so they could serve out the rest of their sentence. Davide was tried under state's determinate sentencing statute.

Paul got 60 years in prison[8], Jennifer got 60 years in prison, and David only did his juvenile term then went on to live as normal a life

---

6.   http://www.nbcdfw.com/news/local/

Affidavits_4_Teens_Planned_To_Kill_N_Texas_Mom.html

7.   http://crimeblog.dallasnews.com/2008/12/roanoke-woman-indicted-in-moth.html/

8.   http://www.apple.com/

as he could have. When police asked Jennifer about her motive, she simply said, "We did not see eye to eye."

It seems like such a small charge for murderers. Would a life-sentence have been more deserved? Probably. Did they get a light charge because they were only kids? Most likely.

My Life of Crime [9] laid out the details in regards to the three murderers. Jennifer Bailey is a white female born on October 5th, 1990. Her maximum sentence date is September, 26th, 2068 which she has been sentenced to spend at Hilltop Unit. Hilltop Unit [10]. is a correctional institutions division (prison) located at 1500 State School Road, Gatesville, TX 76598-2996. It can be found three miles outside of Gatesville.

On The Texas Tribune [11], Jennifer Bailey is listed as being located at the Mountain View Unit for committing "LESSER INCLU MURDER committed on 9/26/2008 in Denton County" for which she is serving a "60-year term" beginning on "9/26/1008."

She is listed as a female, at 25 years of age, found in Mountain View under 01621147, from Denton county, and born 10/5/1990. She is white, 5 ft 5 in, 122 lbs, with blonde hair and hazel eyes.

Her parole eligibility date is 9/26/2038.

On *Denton County, TX Jail Records*, Paul Allen Henson Jr. is listed with the aliases of "Talos, Malaki, and Scai" with an SO# of 164000, and he is described as a white male with brown hair/eyes standing 6'3" at 145 pounds. He was booked at the Denton County Sheriff's Office on 06/09/2009 for capital murder by terror threat/other felony. His offense date is 09/26/2008. Because he has to spend 60 years in jail, he's looking to be released 9/26/2068.

9.　　https://mylifeofcrime.wordpress.com/2012/12/07/kids-that-kill-jennifer-bailey-david-bailey-and-paul-allen-henson-jr/

10.　　https://www.tdcj.state.tx.us/unit_directory/ht.html

11.　　https://www.texastribune.org/library/data/texas-prisons/inmates/jennifer-bailey/727001/

A few years later, Candice Delong sat down in an interview with Jennifer Bailey for the details on Jennifer's perspective that night when they killed Susan Bailey.

During the video,[12] Jennifer says that she went upstairs and started feeling doubtful. She went upstairs to the bathroom and looked at herself good in the face. Jennifer knew she would have to look at that face for the rest of her life and the decision she was about to make.

She questioned if she really wanted to kill her mother. She explained, "That is when I made the decision that I was going to tell my mom what was going to happen and then call the police regardless of the consequences." She then said that she was too late. She heard a scream that broke her thought processes. She went out to the hallway and found her mother pushed up against the wall by Paul who had one hand around her throat and a knife in the other.

Jennifer Bailey then says that her mother told her to "call the police." She adds, "Then I said no."

Explaining why, she said, "Because, at the same time, Paul pointed at me and said, 'Don't!' And to this day, I have no idea why I said, 'no.' After I said, 'no,' Paul just grins and pulls the knife across her throat." From there, Jennifer and David helped finish the mother off. With that, they took off with the mother's car, no money, and whatever gas was in the tank to get them to Canada.

Donna Fielder, the woman who originally covered this story when working at the local newspaper in the Bailey's hometown, recalls the event in September 2008 that ended with the death of Susan Bailey at the hands of four teenagers. She explains how the four of them: Jennifer Bailey, David Bailey, Paul Henson, and Merrilee White tried to kill their parents and steal whatever money they could from them before taking their cars they planned on driving all the way to Canada from Texas.

---

12.   http://www.investigationdiscovery.com/tv-shows/facing-evil/videos/jennifer-bailey/

She recalls that the four teenagers plotted against Susan Bailey, a hard-working mother, and the long journey they made from her death to that run-down gas station they were pulled over at.

Jennifer Bailey, David Bailey, Merrilee White, and Paul Allen Henson enacted one of the most violent crimes in US history to a woman who did not deserve such an attack. It was such a popular case that filmmakers have taken to the story and made video-enactments of it such as *Deadly Women,* a series that took Jennifer Bailey's story and portrayed her as a young girl who fell in love with a pagan, Paul. Paul convinces Bailey to kill her mother and run off with him. They plan on running off to Canada together, but it doesn't quite go as planned. The mother tells her they cannot speak and havoc wreaks as Paul tells Jennifer that she needs to brutally murder her mother.

Susan Bailey was a hard working mother of Jennifer and David who had anything and everything they ever wanted until Paul came into the picture and what they had was just not enough.

Jennifer and Merrilee were bound so tight under the spell of Paul and David just wanted to make his sister happy. With that, they took a sharp blade and took away Susan's life and breath. They tried to get away and enjoy a happy life in the cold of Canada, but they lacked a plan and cash to make that fantasy a truth.

Perhaps this was all the will of a psychopathic teenager who thought he was two people. Sadly, he ruined the lives of two young girls and a young boy to fulfill his disgusting fantasies.

To this day, David and Merrilee sit alone and forgotten and without the ones they loved. Jennifer and Paul await 52 years more of time to stare at bars and cement walls. David lost a sister, a mother, and two friends. Merrilee lost three friends and the trust of her mother. Paul lost two loving parents and both his girlfriends. Jennifer lost the most: her boyfriend who she cared for dearly, her mother, and her self-worth.

The moral of the story? The all-American family, neighbors, children aren't all that movies and books make them be. Darkness taints the pages of every good storybook.

A MOTHER'S KILLER :

THE TRUE STORY OF NICOLE KASINSKAS

CHRISTINE GOODMAN

Nicole Kasinskas was a quiet, unassuming teenage girl. She was born and raised in Nashua, New Hampshire to Anthony Kasinskas and Jeanne Domenico.

"I lived with both of my parents and my younger brother until I was eleven years old," Nicole said. "And my parents divorced and my Dad moved out."

"I think after my parents got divorced and I was dealing with that, I became a little bit angrier. I had a little bit more resentment towards him, and it did change my perspectives about myself and about life in general, I guess even as an eleven year old."

In May of 2002, she found "romance" as a fifteen year old on-line with eighteen-year old Billy Sullivan.

Sullivan lived in a town called Willmantic where he worked as a line cook at McDonald's.

"Nicole hadn't had a lot of boyfriends," prosecuting attorney Kirsten Wilson said . "She was really caught up by the attention by this guy who was saying amazing things to her about how beautiful she was and what she meant to him."

They would communicate daily through e-mail, letters and phone calls. Despite not having met in person, they both declared love for each other within days, speaking of marriage and planning their future together.

"They filled in sort of the gaps of everyday communication and relationships with fantasies and making these assumptions on who the other person was," Wilson said.

"He lived in Connecticut and so our relationship was almost one hundred percent over the phone," Nicole said. "But it became everything to me very quickly because of the amount of attention that he paid me, and I didn't really feel that I was getting that from anywhere else."

Nicole had been vulnerable to Sullivan's Internet advances as she was a loner with very few friends in high school. She was routinely bullied at school by other girls. On one occasion, she was walking down the hall and one of her bullies had pulled her sweatpants down to her ankles. Nicole was not wearing any underwear, furthering the humiliation. Nicole refused to go back to school the next day after that incident.

"The bullying at school certainly made Nicole vulnerable to someone like Sullivan," forensic psychologist Fiona Russo said. "She's lonely, she's being picked on at school and completely humiliated. She stuck to herself and so when some guy pays attention to her, even when it is only online, her fantasy life goes into overdrive. She's able to project things on him that he doesn't deserve or merit."

The more severe the bullying became, the more Nicole began to withdraw and cling to Sullivan.

"As I got older, it was easier for me to isolate from people," Nicole said. "I think at that point I had just gotten used to being more alone as opposed to being around people. And it just became a part of who I was. Maybe if I was more open or maybe if someone had tried harder to reach out, that it could've been different."

Nicole's mom, Jeanne, was her best friend. Jeanne worked at an elementary school for a period of time, holding down such jobs as a crossing guard, a lunchroom monitor, and a paraprofessional for about three years before taking a job where she worked on group contracts for the Benefits, Brokers and Administration department.

"Jeanne Domenico was well loved in the community," Wilson said. "Hard worker. Really sort of a bright, energetic, sweet woman. She was trying to make her daughter happy."

Despite the bullying at school, Nicole got straight A's at school and made her mother happy whenever she made the honor roll.

"School really became my self-worth and I really identified with, like whatever my grades were," Nicole said. "However I was doing in school I felt it reflected on me personally, because I felt that it was so much a part of who I was. I never got in trouble in middle school. I never got spoken to. I never had a detention. It never really crossed my mind to do anything that would be against the rules."

"It would have been helpful if there was more of an acknowledgment that I was doing so well. I think it also would've been helpful if there was more involvement with guidance or something. Just more of a like a check-in...see how things are going."

"Somehow, someway, Nicole got lost in the cracks," Russo said. "That in no way justifies what she did. It may be how she justified it during this time. Her parents are divorced. She doesn't see her Dad. Her mom is working all the time. There had to have been days where she felt intense loneliness Going to school just to be ignored or bullied. To a fourteen year old girl you really may not see the light at the end of the tunnel. So you seek an outlet. Some turn to drugs. Nicole found her own drug in the form of the words that came out of Sullivan's keyboard."

MOTHER AND DAUGHTER TROUBLES

At least on the surface, there were no problems between mother and daughter.

Until Nicole ventured on-line and met Billy Sullivan.

Her mother found out about the relationship and wanting to make her daughter happy, drove the young teenager out to Connecticut so she could meet Sullivan for the first time.

"This was a two hour drive from Nashua to the place in Connecticut where Sullivan lived," Russo said. "It is easy to say here is where Jeanne made a fatal mistake. But in her mind, it is all innocent. Her daughter is fourteen and begging her to drive out to meet this guy. Begging and begging. Until she finally she relents."

More visits followed but friends and classmates knew little of the teen's relationship. Sullivan had informed some of his friends that he had a girlfriend that was "out of state." Other than that, he revealed very little about his personal life.

"He's quiet, he didn't really like to talk," recalled Danny Goss who was a classmate of Sullivan. "But he was good in school and didn't get in any trouble."

"I think the relationship intensified to a degree that Jeanne herself didn't anticipate," Russo said. "And it is easy to play Monday morning quarterback here but there had to have been some kind of father figure present to say 'hey, this is an eighteen-year old working at McDonald's. You are a fourteen year old honor student. You have a future. Don't blow it on this guy. But it isn't like teens listen to you anyway."

The two teenagers soon discussed the prospect of moving in together. Her mother quickly objected to this idea as well as nixing the idea of Nicole sharing a joint bank account with Sullivan.

But the young man later stayed overnight one weekend with Nicole's mother's full consent.

The relationship is the first for Nicole. She pedestalizes Sullivan as everything she has fantasized about is coming true.

"Nicole had a void in her life," Russo said. "When her parents divorced it certainly affected her psychologically in the way she viewed men. Then along comes Sullivan whose older and more experienced. She gets the love from him that perhaps she sought from her father. The older man, wiser than his years, showering her with attention. She was vulnerable to that."

"Her father didn't have too much to do with her after the divorce. She had that longing in her heart for that male figure. And along came Sullivan."

PERSONAL DEMONS OF HIS OWN

Sullivan, however, had his own personal demons he was fighting.

"He did have mental health issues," Wilson said. "He had been hospitalized a number of times. During high school he had some behavioral issues. Some anxiety, that kind of thing."

It was later revealed that Sullivan had been on numerous psychiatric medications to curb his depression, anger and schizophrenia. He had been weaning himself off the meds, however, and on one occasion he engaged in an argument with Nicole's mother over dinner.

Jeanne had asked Billy if she liked the dinner she had prepared. He said yes and then Jean made the comment that "I bet you don't get that too much at home."

Sullivan was highly defensive over anything that involved his home life. When Jeanne made that comment, he turned hostile.

"Sullivan was protective of his home life," Russo said. "If anyone insulted his mother or if he even perceives that someone is insulting his mother then he gets abusive. He did this to Jeanne, who had obviously made nothing more than an idle comment. That was the first warning sign and the relationship should have ended then and there."

Nicole, however, defended her young beau and from that moment the tug of war for her heart began.

"Nicole's own naivete comes to bore at this point," Russo said. "She has no experience with boys and here is this older guy that she looks up to, almost as a father figure of sorts, who turns her against her own family. Against the one person who loved her the most. Her mother. It is a tug of war that the mother loses simply because her daughter's hormones are raging and she doesn't yet have the emotional capacity to know any better."

After a year of dating, in August of 2003, Sullivan drove out to Nashua to spend a week with Nicole. By this time, they are both fed up with Nicole's mother's objections to their ideas of cohabitation.

"Our relationship was definitely emotionally abusive," Nicole said. "And I think now over time, from looking at it, my perspectives on that have changed so much. I feel like he is responsible for his actions and I am responsible for mine. I didn't really get that and I feel like in order to be emotionally abused, in order to stand for it and stay in it, there's gotta be something missing in you. There's gotta be something hurting already, something is not there, something's not right. And that needs to be figured out, found and fixed. Regardless of how a child is acting or what's coming off,there's more inside that kids need help with or guidance or just to have some type of connection with someone. You need to have relationships with people ahead of time, so that when the bad stuff does happen does happen you don't just come in to it expecting to work it out. Like, you need to have firm foundation with that person in order to work it out."

Nicole continued to side with Sullivan against her mother. The two argued constantly, Sullivan's influence quickly become apparent in Nicole's attitude toward her mother as she found fault with everything she did.

The two teens began discussing an unheard of option.

They began discussing the prospect of killing her mother.

"Well, this is where it starts getting...it's a scary business for me," Nicole said in a jailhouse interview. "I'll tell you that. I feel like I"m gonna cry. I don't talk about this stuff so this is really the first time. I think that my relationship with my mom was good. It was fine. I loved my mom. And...that changed. When...I'm not saying I stopped loving my mom, but...our relationship changed. I'm not gonna say that we were the most open because we weren't. We didn't talk about every little thing. I don't remember ever once talking about my parents' divorce with either of them. But the thing is, we didn't really talk about much of anything. When I was fourteen, I became involved with seventeen year old boy. This is really stemming into why I'm here (in jail) now."

OUT OF CONTROL

"Emotions begin to run high as Sullivan ups the ante in his hatred for Nicole's mother," Russo said. "Nicole is emotionally underdeveloped and has to choose between her mother and her 'man.' It is easy to look at it hindsight but with the teenaged girl's warp logic, she sees Sullivan as her entire world now. So she will do anything for him. Even murder."

Nicole's mom really didn't realize the danger that Sullivan was. She began doing what every mom does, demanding that her daughter stop seeing him, stop chatting with him and concentrate on her schoolwork. Nicole, on the other hand, remained fervent in her desire to move to Connecticut to move in with Sullivan.

"Jeanie, rightfully so, said 'you're fifteen you're finishing school,'" Wilson said. "'You're not moving to Connecticut' and that really upset both Nicole and Billy."

The prospect of not seeing Nicole had an adverse emotional effect on Billy.

"He started talking about killing himself...on the road...driving into a big truck because of leaving me..because of his sadness over it," Nicole recalled. "And I think now it just sounds silly, you know? But it wasn't then, and it was terrifying to me because I didn't...I didn't know how to...because of the way that our relationship was. Because he had become so much a part of my life. I mean, I really didn't feel like I was anything without him. I had nothing in my life at that time...I felt...at that time. So the thought of losing him in that way just wasn't okay with me. And that is unfortunately when conversations started about ultimately what happened. I guess I really I don't really go into too many details but I was sixteen and he was eighteen at that time. And I guess I should give you some background. He killed my mom and I was a part of it. I was not physically there but I knew and I helped him. I was, you know, going through the motions of what was being done. But mentally and emotionally, I don't think I was fully there. I don't think I was fully getting it."

"It was emotional manipulation," Russo said. "It is all so scary romantic for a fifteen year old girl to have some guy who is so in love with her that he is going to kill himself because he can't be with her. She has no one in her life to say 'this guy is a loser nutcase.' There isn't anyone that can talk sense to her. So she falls for the emotional manipulation of a highly disturbed but cunning con man."

Billy had convinced the depressed Nicole that her mother was an obstacle to both hers and his happiness.

"I really just did whatever I could to maintain that relationship because I didn't want to lose that," Nicole said. "I didn't want to lose him. And I quickly learned how it would go if I didn't always do everything that he wanted me to do. At that point...you know, getting to be fifteen...sixteen years old...I would fight more with my mom and there was a lot more to fight about, especially with, you know, this relationship that I was having with this kid."

THE FINAL PLAN

The couple tried different methods to murder Jeanne Domenico.

First they tried to poison Jeanne's coffee. The teens had placed Dimetapp, Benadryl and other drugs into Jeanne's coffee creamer in the refrigerator.

Jeanne used the creamer but didn't die and evidently remained ignorant of the plot on her life. The teens then added bleach to the creamer, wanting to strengthen the amount of poison. It was unclear in a court affidavit if Jeanne ever drank from the spiked creamer again.

The next idea was to set Nicole's mattress on fire with a candle. That idea didn't work because the bedding was made of fire retardant material.

It is unclear how the teens planned to fire up the mattress, whether they sneaked into her Nicole's bedroom and tried to fire up the mattress while she slept.

The third idea was to blow up the fuel oil tank in Jeanne's house. The teens had tied two ropes together which would serve as a wick. Their idea was to set fire to the rope which would then ignite a fire from the fuel tank. This idea was of course unsuccessful.

"These were hair-brained schemes from the start," Russo said, "particularly the fuel tank episode. What is interesting is that these are passive attacks. There is no face to face encounter with the mother, they just really want her gone. But it does show how these were test-runs of sorts. Sullivan was working up his nerve to do something violent. Nicole was building up her psyche. With each unsuccessful dry run, their determination and focus to do the job became greater until finally they realized that physical violence would be the only alternative."

THE ATTACK

The couple decided that Sullivan would do the killing. Nicole waited in the car at a local 7-Eleven where he mother worked part time to make ends meet. She wanted to wait there because she hated her home so much. Her boyfriend obliged, and entered the home of Jeanne Domenico between the hours of six and seven in the evening, waiting for her to come home from work.

The plan was for Billy to kill Jeanne by hitting her on the back of her head with a baseball bat.

Nicole waited anxiously in the car for an extended period of time then began to get worried as to why Sullivan was taking so long.

"Nicole called him and asked him what was taking so long," Wilson said. "Jeanne began getting upset that Nicole wasn't home and kept saying 'where is she? Tell her to come home.'"

Nicole heard her mother's voice on the other end of her cell phone telling her to "come home."

As became her habit, she did not listen to her mother.

"Sullivan did not attack Jeanne immediately," Russo said. "Again, he needed that fuel to add to his fire. So he confronted Jeanne, asking her why they kept refusing them to be together. Jeanne would speak logically like any adult would. She's underage. She's still in school. Of course, none of this would get into the head of Sullivan."

Jeanne made the mistake of turning her back on the young man. He then hit her across the back with the baseball bat.

"It looks as if Jeanne tried to get out of the kitchen door," Wilson said. "Billy started grabbing kitchen knives and attacking Jeanne with the steak knives from the state clock in the kitchen."

The attack was, in a word, brutal.

Sullivan stabbed Jeanne numerous times near her heart and stomach. He stabbed with such ferocity that the blade broke off the knife and he had to retrieve another. Then he stabbed her eight times in the throat.

"A number of the steak knives snapped off during the course of the attack," Wilson said.

According to later testimony by Sullivan, Jeanne managed to get a hold of one of the knives and tried to fight back. At this point, however, she is stunned and bleeding. Sullivan realizes that he is in trouble and goes in to finish the job.

Sullivan stabs her repeatedly as Jeanne tries to get away. A blade enters her lung.

"I'm done," were Jeanne's final words.

He then changed his clothes and cleaned the blood off. He then went back to Nicole, telling her to go inside the house to check for any weapons that he may have left behind. He also told her to get a towel.

The murder complete, Sullivan returned to the vehicle and announced that he had done the deal.

The couple, however, had a deal. It was now time for Nicole to do her part. She would help clean up the evidence left behind.

"The fact that she could go and clean up after Billy had killed her mother," Wilson said. "She had to have hit her mother with the door. And then she had to have stepped over her body to clean up for her boyfriend. That she was able to do that was chilling to do me."

Nicole took a cloth and began clean up her mother's blood from the kitchen floor.

"The fact that a psychopath like Sullivan was able to stab Jeanne to death isn't the most blood curdling aspect of this case," Russo said. "The really scary part is how Nicole was able to go back into that house, see her mother laying in a pool of blood on the kitchen floor, then begin to do her end of the bargain, which was to clean up after her boyfriend. The amount of psychological and emotional disconnect here is chilling."

The two then hid the evidence in the outskirts around town before going to a shopping mall in order for Sullivan to purchase new clothes.

Hours after the killing, Nicole finally began to realize the gravity of what has taken place. She realizes that she and Billy were not going off to "see the world." Her best friend, her mother was gone forever.

Jeanne's body would be discovered by her boyfriend later that evening and he quickly called the police. At around 10:15 p.m., Sergeant William Moore and Detective Shawn Hill saw Sullivan and Nicole approach the crime scene.

"They were cocky enough to think they could outwit the cops," Russo said. "By approaching the crime scene and acting all innocent, not knowing what happened, they thought they would deflect attention away from themselves. It really shows you how dumb these two kids were."

The police then stated the teens would have to be separated for an interview. Nicole protested, stating that Sullivan would not know how to get to the police station. The police informed her that they would take him there themselves.

"This is when things start to go haywire in their heads," Russo said. "Nicole is getting nervous, knowing that they will be questioned separately and face the prospect of not having their stories straight. These two were not exactly forward thinking individuals."

The two waited for the police cruisers to arrive and made conversation with Detective Moore. The detective noted that Sullivan did most all of the talking and admitted that he did not like police officers, stating that he had been charged before with crimes he did not commit.

Moore informed Sullivan that he would be given a "fair shake" in the questioning.

Sullivan, however, kept talking. He informed the detective that he had been shopping for souvenirs with Nicole that day and talked about Jeanne's relationship with Nicole. The detective said that Sullivan paced back and forth and then sat down on the trunk of his car.

Twelve minutes later, Detective Linehan arrived on the scene, making contact with both Nicole and Sullivan. Linehan noticed how nervous and "jumpy" Sullivan was. Linehan told Sullivan to "relax" and then the teen explained that he suffered from anxiety but did not need medication. He told the police that he had "no problem" to come to the station for questioning.

Linehan sat with Sullivan in the back seat of the squad car as they headed back to the station. Both of the teens were having casual conversations with the officers but after being questioned separately, they both admitted their involvement, leading police to the locations where they had disposed of the evidence.

"Both of the teenage lovers wilted under the police interrogations," Russo said. "She immediately ratted out Sullivan as the killer while he did the same to her. There was no loyalty for one another while under the police questioning."

Sullivan would be convicted of first degree murder, sentenced to life without parole.

Sullivan, however, did not let his Lothario ways go to rust in jail. He wrote love letters to a girl named Monique Teal who was then sixteen. This occurred while Sullivan was awaiting trial and later Teal's testimony was used in court.

Teal, using a pen name of Monique Sullivan in her love letters to Sullivan, had agreed to a date to marry the now twenty-year old murderer. Teal's mother, however, found out about the letters and forbade him to call or write.

"He just laughed about it," she said. "He said that no matter what my mom would say or do that nothing could keep us away from each other."

"You see him trying the same techniques on Teal," Russo said. "The immediate declarations of love. The flowery language. The idea of them against the world. In Teal's case, however, her mother put a stop to it."

Sullivan admitted to the Jeanne Domenico killing in one of his letters to her, Teal would reveal, although she didn't read from the letter in court. She said she obeyed Sullivan's demands and threw that letter away.

JAIL LIFE

Nicole Kasinskas would plead guilty to second-degree murder.

"My original sentence was forty years to life," Nicole said. "It is now thirty-seven years and a half to life based on a plea that if I acquired my GED I would get two and a half years off. I don't mark days off on my calendar. I don't do those types of things. This is my life now and I want to live it. I don't want to just look at it as one day down closer to my real life. Like this is my real life. I smile a lot and I live a lot and I'm happy a lot and I just prefer it that way rather than get lost in the sadness of it because you can. And I have. But if I...if I can choose not to...if I can be stronger than than then I want to. And it makes me feel freer. It makes me feel that I have more control of my life."

"Her life as a promising honor roll student at fifteen years old with her mother who loved her very much," Wilson said. "She lost her entire life. And for what?"

"I had no goals. I had no hopes and dreams, you know? You need to have your own hobbies and friends and stuff. Outside the relationship, there needs to be that balance. I just never had that, I never figured that out."

"Maybe if someone had said something like, 'I see you, I see that there's more to you than this and I want to see more of you. I'm here for you. I care about you.' I mean everyone needs help, everyone needs support."

BURY THEM ALIVE : THE TRUE STORY OF SERIAL KILLER TIFFANY COLE

JESSICA WINSTON

When James "Reggie" and Carol Sumner moved to Jacksonville, Florida for their retirement, they had visions of good health and happiness. They never thought that their overnight invitation to long-time South Carolina neighbor, Tiffany Cole, would end up the way it did; With the Sumner couple being buried alive.

Reggie and Carol Sumner were high school sweethearts in North Charleston, South Carolina. They were the kind of couple that everyone envied as they walked down the hall. Unfortunately, their lives pulled them in different directions. Reggie decided to serve his country in the navy. After finishing his tour, he got married and landed a job with the railroad. Carol also married and became a devoted mother, however, her first marriage ended in divorce, and her second nearly killed her. In 1987, after years of abuse, her husband at the time shot her seven times in their home before driving away and turning the gun on himself. Her daughter, Rhonda Alford, just ten years old at that time, spent almost a year helping her mother recover from her wounds. She had to help her bathe, dress, and take care of the house. After taking eight years to fully recover, Carol went back to work as soon as she was able. For over twenty-five years she was a civil servant at the Citadel and the Charleston Air Force Base. She also worked a second job at night at a Belk department store, among other jobs she would take when needed. She did whatever she had to in order to make ends meet. Shortly after her recovery, she found out that the blood transfusion she had received during her previous trauma had given her Hepatitis C. She was angry because she felt as though she could not escape her late ex-husband, but she refused to let it ruin her life. She soon started a new job at a cable company and it was during this time that her life finally changed for the better. Nearly forty years after they'd left high school, a chance encounter brought Carol and Reggie together again. One night in 2000, a phone call was made to the cable company where Carol was working, which she received. After talking with the customer Carol and learning his name, she realized that he also sounded just like the Reggie she remembered. So she asked him if he was the same Reggie Sumner who attended Garrett High school in South Charleston. It was. They decided that they should get together after not seeing each other in so long. This time, though they were inseparable. Like "teenagers in love", a quick courtship led to love and then marriage in 2001 with a ceremony at Carol's home in West Ashley. Carol's daughter has said of Reggie "he was just a very gentle, kind and giving spirit. You could not ask for a better friend, husband or stepfather." Eventually, after retiring, the couple decided to move from South Carolina to Jacksonville, Florida. Reggie had previously bought a house during his days working for CSX railroad and as he was a "brittle" diabetic in frail health, he thought he would be more comfortable in the warmer climate. Carol agreed. "She only went down there to honor her husband," Rhonda said. Before moving, they decided to sell their Chevrolet Lumina to the stepdaughter of a friend who lived down the street, Tiffany Cole. They allowed her to make payments on the car to help her out and she agreed, often driving down to Jacksonville with friends to make those payments. Tiffany and the Sumners became friends and Tiffany would often spend the night at their house when she and her friends went down south. A pleasant girl on the outside, the Sumners had no idea what Tiffany could really be like.

Tiffany Ann Cole was born on December 3, 1981, to her sixteen-year-old mother, Shirley Duncan. Her biological father was in jail. She had no male role model to look up to or who could offer her protection the way a father should. Her mother had a boyfriend, but he was beyond cruel and especially loved to torment Tiffany. At one point, she had a puppy which her stepdad threw against a wall, breaking its neck right in front of her. He was abusive verbally as well as physically and Tiffany claims that as a young girl, he began to molest her, beginning around age eight. As a young teenager, she turned to alcohol and drugs to deal with the pain. In high school, Tiffany was a student who participated in cheerleading and played the flute. She was also a girl scout member but eventually the alcohol and drugs took over her life and she quit her programs and dropped out of school. At one point she fell in love with a boy with severe epilepsy, who ended up breaking her heart and since the only example of love from a man came from an abusive stepfather, this breakup reinforced the belief that she should expect to be treated badly and let down by men. She began looking for love in all the wrong places. In May of 2005, during a six-month period of prostitution, Tiffany ran into a man by the name of Michael Jackson. They were drawn to each other right away and began to get high and sleep together.

Michael James Jackson, born May 12, 1982, had a significant criminal history beginning in childhood. Born to a drug-addicted mother, he was mostly raised by his grandmother. He had multiple felony convictions but only for things like fraud and theft. After meeting Tiffany and becoming close, they took a road trip, first going to Myrtle Beach, then driving to Jacksonville, Florida, where they would be staying with Michael's best friend, Alan Wade. Born May 22, 1987, Alan and Michael had known each other for just over a year. When Tiffany and Michael arrived in Florida, they stayed at Alan's mom's house. After just a few days, though, she kicked them out because she was tired of the loud noises and constant partying. With nowhere else to go and with all their money spent on the nights of drinking and partying, Tiffany remembered that the Sumners lived nearby. The three friends showed up at their doorstep and explained what had happened. The couple was very happy to see Tiffany and invited her and her friends to stay the night. While they were chatting and catching up, Carol mentioned how worried they had been about their house in North Carolina not selling. There was no need to worry, however, because not only did their property sell, but they had also made a $99,000 profit. It was this general statement to a long-time neighbor that sealed the Sumner's fate.

It's difficult to know just whose idea it was to rob the Sumner's. Some say it was both Tiffany and Michael, while others say it was Michael who was the plan maker and master manipulator. Either way, a plan was hatched to rob and kill the loving couple. At some point in June, Alan had contacted his friend, Bruce Nixon Jr., and told him of a plan to rob someone. No other details were given. Then on July 6th, Alan called Bruce, born May 9th, 1987, and asked him if he would be interested in joining the others in digging a hole. Bruce agreed and stole four shovels from his neighborhood. The other three friends drove to Bruce's house in a rented Mazda RX-8 that Tiffany had rented in South Carolina. The group drove around hoping to find a perfectly remote place for the hole to be dug. Alan asked Bruce if he knew of any good places to which Bruce responded that he did. He took them into Georgia, to a wooded area just over the state line. Leaving the car parked on the road, the group walked through the wooded area into a clearing where they began to dig a hole while Tiffany held a flashlight. It was approximately four feet deep and six feet square. Upon completion of the hole, they left the shovels and went back to the car. It was here that Alan asked Michael if Bruce could join in on their robbery plan. Michael agreed. The foursome drove back to Alan's house but his mother would not allow Michael in as she believed him to be a bad influence on her son. Over the next couple of days, it was

Tiffany's job to remain in contact with Carol and Reggie in order to gain information from them about their plans and whereabouts. The foursome also secretly watched the house in order to figure out the Sumner's routine. It was unclear yet as to whether or not the group would enter the home while the couple was gone or if they would simply go in with the couple there. It was ultimately decided that they would enter the home while the couple was there so that they could get their financial information and the means to access their accounts. Michael said that he would kill the victims by injecting them with a lethal dose of their medications. He then promised that the four friends would split the money they received from the Sumner's accounts, each receiving about $50,000. They began making preparations for their plan. Just after midnight on July 8th, 2005, Michael, Tiffany, and Alan went to Wal-Mart and purchased disposable rubber gloves. On the evening of the murders, they went to an Office Depot, where Tiffany bought duct tape and a large roll of plastic wrap. Last, they bought a toy gun that shot plastic pellets.

Around 10pm., on July 8th, 2005, Tiffany drove the other three group members to the Sumner's house in the Mazda. Herself and Michael remained in the car while Alan and Bruce went up to the door. They had the duct tape and toy gun and both were wearing the plastic gloves. After Carol answered the door, Bruce and Alan told her that they were having car trouble and asked if they could use their phone. Carol said of course they could and invited them in. As soon as the boys entered the home, Alan pulled the phone cord out of the wall. Bruce pointed the gun at the couple. Alan grabbed Reggie around the neck and pushed him down into a chair. They told the couple that they wanted credit and debit cards and any other financial information. Carol began pleading with the boys not to hurt them. Bruce took the couple into a spare bedroom where he used duct tape to bind their legs and hands and to cover their mouths and eyes. Alan sent a text message to Michael, informing him that everything was under control. Michael then also entered the home and he and Alan began searching for financial information. They saw a pile of mail and financial statements which they put into a plastic bag. They spotted Reggie's prized coin collection and took that too. Michael told the other two to take the couple into the garage at which point they put them into the trunk of the Lincoln Town car. Tiffany went into the house and grabbed some of their belongings, put them into a bag and took the bag with her to the Mazda. Following the plan, both cars headed towards the gravesite, stopping only once to put gas in the Lincoln. Upon arrival at the site, Michael opened the trunk and apparently began screaming when he saw that the duct tape had become loose and the couple had worked the tape off. It had been over 100 degrees in the trunk. Sweat had caused the tape to loosen. They had also taken the tape off their eyes and were huddled together. Michael ordered Bruce to tape them up again, which he did. Alan then attempted to back up the car to the edge of the grave but, unable to do so, Bruce took over. Michael then sent Bruce up the road to wait with Tiffany at the Mazda. While still alive, the Sumners were taken out of the trunk and pushed into the hole. It is unclear as to who actually did the burying because Alan and Michael each blamed the other. Somehow, Michael ended up getting the personal identification number of the Sumner's bank account. Reports differ on whether he obtained this information from somewhere in the house or if Carol told him the number while being threatened to be buried alive. According to one documentary, Carol had gotten the tape off her mouth again when in the hole. Michael was telling them that if they didn't give up their PIN, they would die, at which point Carol yelled it out. It didn't seem to matter either way though because they continued to shovel dirt onto the scared couple.

After filling the hole, Alan and Michael put the shovels back into the trunk of the Lincoln and drove it up the road to where Tiffany and Bruce were waiting with the Mazda. The four of them drove to

Sanderson, Florida, where they abandoned the Lincoln after wiping it clean of fingerprints. They then drove back to Jacksonville where they immediately went to an ATM and withdrew money from the Sumner's account, before retiring to a hotel. Alan and Tiffany went to another Wal-Mart where they purchased more latex gloves as well as bleach. They returned to the Sumner's home in order to clean up any evidence. They also stole a computer. Bruce stayed with the group for another day and then went home, but Alan remained with Michael and Tiffany who returned to South Carolina, where Tiffany rented two hotel rooms; one for herself and Michael and one for Alan. It should be noted that after returning home, Bruce went to a party with a plastic bag filled with different medications. At one point he announced that he had found a new job murdering people. He stated that he had buried people alive and killed them without mentioning the involvement of anyone else.

On the morning of July 10th, Carol's daughter, Rhonda, decided to report to police the fact that she hadn't been able to get hold of her mother for a few days. Since they kept in touch on a regular basis and spoke every couple days, it was highly unusual for her mother to not return her calls. The next day, the Jacksonville Sheriff's Office (JSO) went to the Sumner's home. The back door of the house was unlocked and in the kitchen there dirty after-dinner plates, which was also highly unusual for the couple. The JSO began to investigate the financial accounts of the couple and they found that large amounts of money had been withdrawn within a short time frame. Video footage from the ATM machines that the group had used showed Michael's face and the silver Mazda in the background. On July 12th, after Rhonda made a plea on local TV networks for the safe return of her parents, the Sheriff's office received a phone call from someone posing as Reggie Sumner. Dispatch contacted Detective David Meacham of the Sheriff's office and put the caller through.

Meacham: Where are you at?

Michael: We're in Delaware right now

Meacham: And what city is that in?

Michael: It's in Corpus

Meacham: Corpus, Delaware?

Michael: Yes

However, the town of Corpus, Delaware does not exist. Next, Tiffany came on the phone posing as Carol.

Meacham: Is this Carol?

Tiffany: Yes, sir, it is.

Meacham: Okay. This is Detective Meacham from the Sheriff's office. How are you doing tonight?

Tiffany: I was sleeping

Meacham: I understand. I understand you have some health problems

Tiffany: Mmhmm

Meacham: Okay. Any other problems?

Tiffany: I'm really tired right now

Meacham: What kind of problems do you have?

Tiffany: Cancer

Meacham: Cancer?

Tiffany: Mmhmm

The detective called Rhonda into the station so that she could listen to the taped conversation. She confirmed that the people posing as the Sumners were definitely not Carol and Reggie. The main reason for the call was to ensure everyone that the Sumners were alive and well and because the bank accounts had been frozen. They asked the detectives to reinstate the accounts, which they did so that they could track the money in order to locate the perpetrators. They also had the phone number from which Michael had called. Using this information, they were able to find that the phone was registered to Michael and that a call had been placed to a car rental agency in Charleston. They also learned that the cell had been used near the Sumner's home the night of the murders. Detective Meacham contacted the rental company and was told that the car had been rented to a Tiffany Cole and that it was overdue. Using the rental car's GPS system, they were able to find that the car had also been near the Sumner's residence during the time of the abduction. Using the cell phone trace, the car's GPS and the photos of Michael at different ATMs, police were able to locate the general whereabouts of the three murderers. On July 14th, with help from Tiffany's brother, who was on probation and threatened with jail, police raided a Best Western hotel in Charleston and arrested Tiffany Cole, Alan Wade, and Michael Jackson. Bruce Nixon was also picked up at his home in Florida.

While Tiffany, Michael, and Alan refused to cooperate with law enforcement, Bruce appeared to have some semblance of a conscience because he broke down and admitted to the crimes right away. He also agreed to lead police to the burial site. For the first time in TV history, documentary footage showed Bruce and detectives at the grave site where Bruce broke down in sobs. Excavation of the site began the next day. The victims were found fully clothed in a crouching position. Reggie had somehow broken his tape and was holding Carol's hand. There was two feet of dirt over their heads. With ten years of homicide under his belt, Detective Meacham said it was one of the saddest and most horrible things he had ever seen. The medical examiner determined that both Reggie and Carol were alive in the hole before they were buried. Their nostrils, mouths, throats, esophagi, and trachea had fine sprays of dirt in them, which indicated that they had inhaled it. They died from mechanical asphyxiation and smothering, caused by the dirt covering their heads while compressing their chests. She said it was the worst case of asphyxiation she'd ever seen. It was "horrendous."

At some point while in jail, but unaware that Bruce had come clean, Michael's grandmother called him.

Grandma: Michael, listen to me and don't say a word. You're in the newspaper. All over the newspaper yesterday and today

Michael: For what?

Grandma: Murder

Michael: What?!

Grandma: Murder. 'Bodies ID'd as former South Carolina couple James and Carol Sumner. Bail was denied for 18-year-old Bruce Nixon of Florida who was arrested and charged with murder, home invasion, robbery, and kidnapping.' He took them to the grave site and everything

Michael: Oh my God. Are you kidding me?

Grandma: It's right here in today's paper

Michael: Bruce took them to the f*****g spot. The f****r showed them where the spot was at?

Grandma: Yes, dear

Michael: *starts panting* Bruce just killed us all

Bruce Nixon told detectives everything that had happened and agreed to testify on behalf of the prosecution. He wasn't sentenced until after he testified against the other three group members, but in the end, he received 45 years for each victim, currently being served concurrently at Century Correctional Institution in Florida. Alan Wade was tried first.

Michael Jackson was the first to be tried. Testifying on his own behalf, Michael stated that the plan was only to rob the Sumners and that it was not going to involve murder. He said that Alan and Bruce went into the house and when they came out they drove off in the Lincoln which he then followed. He claims he had no idea that Reggie and Carol were in the trunk. According to Michael, when they arrived at the hole in Georgia, it was Alan and Bruce who told him where to park and to bring them a flashlight. It was when he arrived at the burial site that he heard Carol moan. He then stated that he questioned what the other two were doing before returning to the Mazda to wait. He did admit to impersonating Reggie. Bruce testified that Michael had been the ringleader and was the one who orchestrated everything.

After stepping down from the witness stand, Carol's daughter, Rhonda, said of Bruce, "I just wanted to hug him. He is a murderer, but in the end, he did the right thing." It was that testimony that she believed sealed Michael's fate because he was found guilty of first degree murder, robbery, and kid-napping, and sentenced to death for each murder. He is currently on death row in Florida.

Alan was next to be tried. Two witnesses who were not identified gave victim impact statements during the penalty phase. Alan's lawyer then called six of their own witnesses to testify including Bruce Nixon, Alan's mom and sister, the mother of a friend, his middle school principal, and his youth pastor. Overall, the witnesses testified that Alan's parents divorced when he was eight and his father disappeared from his life. His mother took him to church regularly and as a kid, he was kind, smart, and well-behaved. After the divorce, his mother was unable to spend a lot of time with him because she had to work a lot to support them. When he was in his teens, his mother had a bout with breast cancer. By his early teens, he began to use drugs. In the sixth grade, he was involuntarily committed to a 72-hour hold because of a drug related incident. When he was sixteen, his mom had to take him out of school or be arrested for his truancy. The next year, his mother kicked him out of the house in an attempt at tough love because his drug use was becoming worse. In 2004 Alan introduced her to Michael, whom she immediately saw as a bad influence on him. Since his arrest and before his trial, Alan had apparently become a model prisoner, obtained his G.E.D and tutored other inmates in math. Nothing seemed to sway the jury, however, because he was found guilty on all counts and voted eleven-to-one to receive the death penalty. He is also currently on death row in Florida.

Tiffany was the last to be tried. Her lawyer argued that she wasn't a major participant in the crimes. He said that she was under the control of her boyfriend Michael, and that he was the mastermind. Tiffany claimed that she believed the crime would only constitute a simple theft and that she didn't knowingly participate in the robberies, kidnapping or murders. She insisted that she did not know that Reggie and Carol were in the trunk of the Lincoln until they arrived at the burial site. The circuit judge, Michael Weatherby did not see it that way, stating that it was she who held the flashlight during the digging of the grave and was there when they were bound and placed in the trunk. He also noted that she was the one who purchased the duct tape and gloves and later pawned the jewelry and computer they had stolen. "She was thoroughly involved," Weatherby stated. "She knew exactly what she was doing and participated without hesitation." It was noted as well that she was the only one of the four who had previously known the Sumners. During the penalty phase, the prosecution called two of the victim's family members who gave impact statements. The defense attorney then called up witnesses who testified that Tiffany was of good character. Three of those witnesses were correctional officers who stated that Tiffany had been no trouble in jail and did not cause any problems. A psychiatrist, Dr. Earnest Miller, testified that she suffered from poly-substance and alcohol abuse, chronic depression, and a personality disorder. He also stated that she had witnessed abuse to family members and had been sexually abused herself by her stepfather. On the other hand, he testified that Tiffany was competent and thus he could not support a plea of insanity. Finally, he stated that she knew right from wrong and had a high average IQ. In the end, Tiffany was also found guilty of all charges and sentenced to death by a 9-3 vote. Upon hearing her fate, she bowed her head and turned to her mother, mouthing the words "I love you". Her lawyer, Quentin Till, said she had been ready for the decision. He visited her in jail that week. "I told her to be strong," he said. "...I still see her being utilized and manipulated by Michael Jackson." Revis Sumner, Reggie's brother, said that Tiffany has since written to the family, asking for forgiveness. He says he has forgiven her, but that doesn't mean she shouldn't suffer for her actions. The Reverend Jean Clark, Reggie's sister has said, "I pray for Tiffany.

I pray for all of them. I'm grieved that these four young people have wasted their lives." Chief Assistant State Attorney, Jay Plotkin, who tried all four cases said, "All of these defendants got exactly what they deserved. Justice was done." After the sentences were given and the trials were over, Reggie's son, Frederick Hallock, said, "You expect some sort of closure or some sort of good feeling when the verdict is read, but it didn't seem to help much. I just know they didn't deserve this." Currently, Tiffany is one of only five women on Florida's death row. At the time of her sentence, she was the sole woman there.

Tiffany, Michael, and Alan all filed appeals after their trials, citing multiple issues. All three were denied and their sentences were upheld. Recently, in 2015, Tiffany filed another appeal, asking for a new trial. She claims that her defense lawyers were ineffective and that she should not have been convicted of first-degree murder since she did not actually bury the bodies herself. But according to Florida law, it doesn't matter who actually committed the murder. Just knowing that it was going to happen is enough to warrant a guilty verdict. At her original trial Tiffany said, "But please remember I didn't do this. I am not the monster that created this, but I regret meeting him," referring to Michael. Upon hearing that Tiffany was asking for a new trial, Reggie's sister, Jean had this to say: "Most people are going to try to come back with something like that after the fact, because they're going to try to find a loophole and get off. But justice has a voice, and justice has to be served." And the thought of going through another trial breaks her heart. "I have family members that are still not the same and never will be the same. In fact, I don't like to involve them too much into things like this, because they can't deal with it."

In 2014, Alan Wade also filed an appeal for a new trial, citing that his lawyers did not do a good job of representing him. His appellate lawyers said that his original defense lawyers barely met with him before the trial and didn't interview witnesses prior to putting them on the stand. They also cited the lack of objections to supposedly questionable evidence. In December 2014, it was decided by the Supreme Court of Florida that his conviction be upheld.

Previous to that, Michael Jackson filed an appeal for a new trial, stating that his lawyers were also ineffective. As with Alan's trial, Michael claims that his lawyers did not make objections to certain evidence when there was clearly an objection to be made. The judge did allow an appeal hearing for his concerns and at the close of the hearing, Michael was allowed to make a statement. It went as follows:

First, I'd like to say that I am guilty of the crimes of first-degree murder, kidnapping, and robbery against Mr. and Mrs. Sumner. My reason for wanting to address the Court today is because of the many lies I told to everyone years ago at pretrial and then trial. I downplayed my involvement to look as if I were not guilty but the truth is that—the truth is that it was my idea to do this. Truly, I did not make anyone do anything. All were willing participants but I was, in fact, the leader. It was my idea to do it. I lied to this Court all throughout my trial testimony, same to [defense counsel and the State]. Even more so I lied to the people who deserve the truth the most, the family of Mr. and Mrs. Sumner, and for that, I am deeply sorry. There are no words that I could ever offer that would convey the depth of my remorse or sorrow, but again I say that I am truly sorry for what I have done and though I'm undeserving, I do ask forgiveness. My desire today is to reconcile the truth to the family of Mr. and Mrs. Sumner and to Your Honor, the attorneys and to the Court record. If necessary, I will answer any and all questions fully and truthfully. Thank you.

His conviction was upheld. Tiffany, Michael, Alan, and Bruce remain in jail today, with the former three on death row.

"It's sad," said Rhonda Alford about her parents. "It took them so long to find each other." Carol and Reggie's ashes sit in an urn in Rhonda's home, forever mixed and blended together.